THE
JEWISH CHILD'S
BIBLE STORIES

TOLD IN SIMPLE LANGUAGE

By
ADDIE RICHMAN ALTMAN

ILLUSTRATED

Kessinger Publishing's Rare Mystical Reprints

THOUSANDS OF SCARCE BOOKS ON THESE AND OTHER SUBJECTS:

Freemasonry * Akashic * Alchemy * Alternative Health * Ancient Civilizations * Anthroposophy * Astrology * Astronomy * Aura * Bible Study * Cabalah * Cartomancy * Chakras * Clairvoyance * Comparative Religions * Divination * Druids * Eastern Thought * Egyptology * Esoterism * Essenes * Etheric * ESP * Gnosticism * Great White Brotherhood * Hermetics * Kabalah * Karma * Knights Templar * Kundalini * Magic * Meditation * Mediumship * Mesmerism * Metaphysics * Mithraism * Mystery Schools * Mysticism * Mythology * Numerology * Occultism * Palmistry * Pantheism * Parapsychology * Philosophy * Prosperity * Psychokinesis * Psychology * Pyramids * Qabalah * Reincarnation * Rosicrucian * Sacred Geometry * Secret Rituals * Secret Societies * Spiritism * Symbolism * Tarot * Telepathy * Theosophy * Transcendentalism * Upanishads * Vedanta * Wisdom * Yoga * *Plus Much More!*

DOWNLOAD A FREE CATALOG AND SEARCH OUR TITLES AT:

www.kessinger.net

MOSES AND THE TEN COMMANDMENTS

FOREWORD

In launching this little volume upon the sea of juvenile literature, I would say that I have taught the younger children of Sabbath and Mission Schools for many years, but found very few books of Bible Stories to assist me. Many of these books are written by non-Jews, non-Jewish applications are made, and non-Jewish views either implied or asserted. Even when written by Jews, the stories seem intended for older children, and are consequently beyond the mental capacity of the little ones.

I therefore began to tell these stories in my own way, with but one end in view—to bring the ethical side of the Bible into equal prominence with the religious thoughts. The results were gratifying. I drew no moral, but told the stories in such simple language that very young children could unconsciously deduct their own inferences.

I have made no endeavor in either style or phraseology to give this book any value from a purely literary standpoint. On the contrary, the language is limited to a child's vocabulary and adapted to the comprehension of a child, consequently many repetitions of the same words and of the same thoughts occur. My sole aim has been to make these old, yet ever new, stories so attractive to the children, that each one will hold their attention and interest from beginning to end. Thus subconsciously, with no effort on the part of the little ones, the Bible heroes and heroines will become as familiar to them, and as dear, as those of history, mythology and fiction. The illustrations were selected with particular care, for the child absolutely requires

FOREWORD

assistance of the physical eye to thoroughly comprehend and absorb any story.

In a few instances I have taken the author's privilege to emphasize the ethical value at a slight expense of accuracy, but I trust no one will take exception to this.

I also wish to give credit for the story of the "Charity Trumpet" in the outer court of the Temple of Solomon, to Mr. Louis Schnabel. He was once the superintendent of the Hebrew Orphan Asylum of New York City, and was a man thoroughly versed in the tales of the Midrash and Talmud.

ADDIE RICHMAN ALTMAN.

CONTENTS

I.	THE GARDEN. Adam and Eve	7
II.	TWO BOYS. Cain and Abel	13
III.	THE GREAT RAIN. Noah	20
IV.	THE VISIT OF THE ANGELS. Abraham	27
V.	THE RAM ON THE MOUNTAIN. Isaac	34
VI.	THE BROTHERS. Esau and Jacob	41
VII.	THE DREAMER. Joseph	49
VIII.	THE GOVERNOR OF EGYPT. Joseph	56
IX.	THE BABY IN THE BASKET. Moses	66
X.	THE GREAT LEADER. Moses	78
XI.	THE WOMAN JUDGE. Deborah	88
XII.	A STORY OF LOVE. Ruth	92
XIII.	THE BOY PRIEST. Samuel	99
XIV.	THE SHEPHERD KING. David	105
XV.	THE WISE KING. Solomon	115
XVI.	THE MAN OF GOD. Daniel	125
XVII.	THE STORY OF CHANUKKAH	133
XVIII.	THE STORY OF PURIM	141

ILLUSTRATIONS

Moses and the Ten Commandments	Frontispiece
Adam and Eve Leave the Beautiful Garden	8
Cain and Abel Offering Sacrifice	16
Noah Leaving the Ark	24
The Angels Promise a Child to Abraham	30
The Sacrifice of Isaac	36
Isaac Gives Jacob his Blessing	44
Joseph Sold by his Brothers	52
Joseph Makes Himself Known to his Brothers	64
The Baby Boy Moses Hidden in the Bulrushes	68
Moses Presenting the Ten Commandments to the People of Israel	84
Deborah	88
Ruth, throwing her arms around Naomi, said: "Entreat me not to leave thee."	94
Hannah Brings her Little Boy Samuel to Eli	100
David Playing the Harp before King Saul	110
"Oh, Great King, do not cut my child in two," cried the real mother to Solomon	116
Daniel in the Den of Wild Lions	128
Judas Maccabeus	136
Esther Before the King	146

The Jewish Child's Bible Stories

I

THE GARDEN

ADAM AND EVE

Once upon a time, many, many years ago, there was a beautiful garden, in a land very far away from here. All the nicest plants you can think of, and trees, and bushes, and grass, grew in this garden, which was just like a big park. There were very tall trees covered with bright green leaves, and other trees loaded with every kind of fruit,—apples and pears, peaches and plums, and oranges and bananas.

On the bushes there grew pineapples and berries, and low down in the grass, pretty red strawberries peeped out from under the little leaves. Then there were flowers, oh! such lovely flowers, that seemed to grow everywhere—red roses, and white ones, and yellow ones, and carnations, and violets, and pansies, and buttercups, and honeysuckle, and every other kind of flower.

There was also a wide river, that flowed along through the garden. The river wound in and out among the trees, and if you had been there, you could have seen hundreds of fishes swimming in the water. There were big ones, and little ones, and black, and white, and red, and yellow ones too, that could be seen in the clear, cool water.

Don't you think that was the loveliest garden you ever heard about? And there were other things there, too. Birds were singing in the trees and some animals were lying on the ground. Some of the animals were running or walking around, and a man and a woman were there. The man's name was Adam, and the woman's name was Eve.

Do you know, or can you guess who made this lovely garden; and all the things in it? It was the dear, good God, who takes care of us all—our Father in Heaven. He made the garden, and the river, and He made the fish, and the birds, and the animals.

And He gave everything to Adam and Eve. God told Adam and Eve they could live in the garden, God also told them they could give names to the trees, and flowers, and to all the living things.

ADAM AND EVE LEAVE THE BEAUTIFUL GARDEN

THE GARDEN

Adam and Eve were as happy as little children are when they get a nice present, for all these beautiful things in the garden were a present from God. But God told them there was one fine tree, in the middle of the garden, which they must not touch.

And God said to Adam and Eve: "You may eat of all the fruit that grows in the garden, except from this one tree. This tree is my own. Do not forget what I have said, and do not touch it."

Adam and Eve thought God was very good to give them so many things. They made up their minds never to touch God's tree, even though they could see the big red apples that were on it.

For many days, Adam and Eve were kept pretty busy thinking about the names they would give to everything.

At last, all the living things had names, and the flowers and trees, too. Adam and Eve were kind and gentle, and the animals and birds, and even the fish, loved Adam and Eve, and they would run, or fly, or swim to them whenever they were called, just as your dog or kitty comes to you.

The happy times kept on until one day, when something dreadful happened. Adam had gone away to the other side of the river, to get some peaches that grew over there. Eve was walking around by herself. She was near the middle of the garden, very near to God's tree, the tree with the ripe, red apples. Eve stopped in the road, looked at them for a long time, and then said:

"How nice those apples look! Don't I wish I could have just one!"

Just at that instant she heard a queer, hissing noise near her. She looked around, and saw a large snake, or serpent, coiled upon a bush near by. The serpent looked right into Eve's eyes, and said:

"Why don't you take one, then, if you want it so much? Nobody will see you."

And then—just think of it! Eve was so naughty, she picked an apple from God's tree, and took a bite! Wasn't she foolish to believe what that snake said, to believe that nobody saw her? We know who saw her, and who knew what she had done, don't we?

After Eve had taken a few little bites, she began to feel sorry. And she was so ashamed of herself because she had disobeyed, that she did not know what to do.

THE GARDEN

She was afraid, too, and ran quickly to look for Adam. When she found him, she told him what she had done, and handed him the apple to take some, too. Adam said:

"Oh, Eve, how could you have been so bad, when God has beeen so good to us? Now I am sure we will be punished."

Eve began to cry, for she was very unhappy, just like children are when they have been naughty, and are afraid their papa will punish them.

"Anyhow, it was not my fault," said Eve. "I would not have touched the apple, but the old serpent told me to, and you can blame him. I suppose you might eat some of it now, as long as I did."

And then Adam was just as naughty as Eve. He ate some of the apple, and afterwards he was just as ashamed and as unhappy as Eve. They were both so scared they tried to hide themselves. They found a place behind some very thick and tall bushes, and they thought God could not find them. But God sees everything. God knew what they had done, and He called:

"Adam and Eve, where are you?"

At first they did not answer, but when God said:

"I see you, Adam and Eve," they came out of their hiding place.

God was very sad when He looked at them, and He said:

"I am very sorry to punish you, but you did not obey me. So you must leave my beautiful garden. You must go away from here, and you will have to work to get your food. You can never come back again, Adam and Eve, for I cannot trust you."

Adam and Eve were very sorry then, because they had not obeyed, and because God could not trust them any more. They had to leave the garden at once, for God sent an angel to take them away. After they were gone, the angel stayed by the gate to see that they never came back.

And God told the wicked serpent, who was the cause of all the trouble in the garden, that he must be punished, too. His punishment was that he could never walk like the other animals. And to this day, all the serpents have to crawl on the ground, instead of walking on feet.

II

TWO BOYS

CAIN AND ABEL

After Adam and Eve left the garden where they had been so happy, they wandered around, outside of it. They were very sorry they had been so naughty, but that did not help them. They began to look for some place where they could live. They found a cave near a big, shady, tree, and they thought this would be a good house. They began to work, and tried to be happy, but they often thought of the lovely garden, and wished they had obeyed.

One day, a little baby boy came to Adam and Eve. They named him Cain, and when another little fellow came along later, they called him Abel. Cain was two years older than Abel, and he was very different from him. Cain had dark hair and black eyes, and was a big, strong baby, and Abel had light hair and blue eyes, and was not very strong.

From the time they were both little children, they were

very different in everything they did. Cain always looked cross, and angry, and miserable, and Abel was cheerful, and sweet, and happy. Their parents had to work very hard, and the little boys often had to help their mother.

When Eve would call Cain, and tell him to bring some wood, or clean up the yard, or go somewhere for her, Cain would say in a cross voice:

"Oh, dear! I don't want to work. I don't like to do things," and when she made him do it he would get very angry.

Whenever she called Abel, he would come running and say in a cheerful way:

"Yes, mother, dear, I will help you," and he would go quickly and do it well.

Cain always thought every one was "down on him," but that was not true. He was so cross all the time that he only thought so. Haven't you often heard children say that? They say some one is "down on them," but it is not very true. It is nearly always the child's own fault.

When Cain and Abel grew up, their father said to them one day:

"You are both big enough to work all day now, so you must help me. You, Abel, are not very strong, so you can take care of the sheep and goats. You must watch them all day, so they don't run away or get lost. And you, Cain, can come out into the fields with me. You can help plant the corn, and take care of the fruit trees."

So the boys began to work, and every day they left home early in the morning. It was just the same as before, for Cain was always cross and ugly, no matter what he had to do; and Abel was happy as he could be, caring for the animals, whether it was hot or cold, or rainy, or fine weather. And so the years passed away.

One evening, in the fall of the year, after all the grain and fruit were ripe, and when the little baby lambs and goats had grown quite large, Adam said to the boys:

"God has given us fine weather, with plenty of sunshine and plenty of rain. All the seeds that we planted, came up as we wanted them. The grain and fruit are ripe. Our sheep and goats are well and tomorrow we will show God that we are thankful to Him for all His kindness. I want you to get up early tomorrow morning, boys, and I will show you what to do."

In those times, there were no temples, or churches, where people prayed to God, and really the people did not know how to pray. But way down in their hearts, they felt they must show in some way that they loved God—so listen to what they did. They went into the fields to look for a large, flat stone. Then they picked up sticks and laid them back and forth across the stone, till they had a big pile of wood.

They called this stone with all the sticks piled on it, an altar. Then they brought the best fruit and grain that they had, and a little goat or lamb, and laid all on the altar, and set fire to the wood. This was called a sacrifice. The people thought God would notice the sweet smell of the sacrifice, and that He would be glad.

Cain and Abel each built an altar. Abel was very particular to have every piece of wood quite dry, so it would burn well. He was very careful to pick up sticks that were straight, and he laid them evenly. But Cain was cross and angry, like he always was when he had to do anything. He picked up all kinds of sticks, long and short, and wet and crooked, and he laid them very carelessly on the stone.

When the two altars were finished, the boys went

CAIN AND ABEL OFFERING SACRIFICE

TWO BOYS

away to get the sacrifice. Abel took his dearest little lambkin and baby goat, killed them and put them on his altar. Cain brought grain and fruit, and placed them on his altar. Then they set fire to the wood, and stood near by to watch it burn.

You should have seen how differently those two fires burned! On Abel's altar the flames burned brightly, and the smoke rose up in a tall, straight line, nearly up to the clouds. Abel was very glad, for he thought to himself that God liked his sacrifice. You see, Abel had done everything carefully, and whatever we do carefully turns out well.

But how was it with Cain? There he stood, doubling up his fists at the fire, which was burning very badly. He was angry when he saw how well Abel's fire burned, and he thought that even the fire was "down on him." Wasn't that foolish when it was all his own fault? He had brought wet wood, and was careless in piling it up, and so he spoiled his fire himself.

Cain grew more angry every minute, and soon went away. Abel waited till his fire was out, and then started to look for his brother. Abel was sorry to see how unhappy Cain always made himself by the foolish things he did, so when he saw Cain in the next field he went towards him to speak to him. But Cain would not listen. He told Abel to keep still, and then—he struck him!

Cain was so strong, he did not know how heavy and hard he could strike. When he saw how Abel fell down and did not get up again, he was frightened. He bent down to look into Abel's face, and saw that he was dead. Cain surely did not mean to kill his own brother, but he was so angry he did not know what he was doing.

Just think how Cain must have felt! He started to run away before any one could find out what he had done, or before any one could see him. But Cain forgot there is Some One who always sees us, and who always knows what we do. Cain heard a Voice calling to him:

"Cain, where is your brother Abel?" and Cain answered:

"I am not my brother's keeper." (He meant that he did not have to take care of his brother.)

Then God said: "I know what you did to your brother. I know how bad and wicked you are, and I will punish you. You must go far away from here, and you shall never, never have a home again."

So Cain had to leave his father and mother. Cain lived to be a very old man, but he could not forget what he had done to his brother, and he was very unhappy all his life.

III

THE GREAT RAIN

NOAH

Many, many years passed away, and many children were born. They grew up, and married, and had more children, and there was a large number of people in the world. But these people were not very good, and they were very lazy. They did not want to work, and the only thing they thought about was to have a good time. They forgot all about the good God, and they often did wicked things.

But there was one man, named Noah, and his family, who were good, and loved God, and who always tried to do what is right. God, who sees and hears everything, knew how bad the other people were, and God felt He must punish them, just like papas and mammas punish their children when they have been naughty.

God knew that Noah and his family were good, so, of course, He would not punish them. One day God called to Noah and said:

THE GREAT RAIN

"Noah, all the people around here are very wicked. They do so many naughty things, and they make each other so unhappy, that I must punish them. But you, Noah, and your family have always been good, so I will not punish you."

Then God told Noah that he and his sons should build a very large boat with a strong roof on top, and cover it with tar and pitch, so that no water could get inside. And God said:

"When it is finished, I will tell you what else you must do."

Noah called his three sons, Shem, Ham and Japheth, and the four men went into the forest together. They took heavy axes with them, and cut down some tall, strong trees. They chopped and sawed and hammered, day after day, from morning till night. It was very hard work, but, after a long time, the great big boat was finished.

It was not a bit like the boats they have now. This one was more like a house, for it had high walls, and a slanting roof, and it was black as ink; for it was painted all over with tar and pitch, so that no water could get inside. This boat was called an ark, and because Noah and his sons built it, it was called "Noah's Ark."

Then God spoke to Noah again. He said: "Now go and get all the food you can find, for your family, and for all the living things that you must take into the ark. I am going to send a great rain," said God, "and it will rain so much that all the wicked people will be washed away, and the world will be clean again."

Then God told Noah that after he put the food into the ark, Noah should collect animals and birds and insects, and after they were safe in the ark, the rain would begin. Noah and his sons had a great time gathering all the living things together, but at last, there they stood, two by two, in long, long lines.

There were camels, elephants, lions, bears, tigers, wolves, foxes, deer, goats, sheep, donkeys, oxen, cows, dogs, horses, squirrels, snakes, and mice; ostriches, chickens, eagles, sparrows, storks, ravens, and doves; frogs, locusts, caterpillars, ants, flies, turtles, bees, lizards, and worms, and all the other living things you can think about.

And just try to think how long it took to catch so many animals, and to get them all in line ready to go

THE GREAT RAIN

into the ark; for there were two pairs of some kinds of birds and animals and insects, and seven pairs (14) of other kinds of the living things. They all marched into the ark, into the cages Noah had made for them, and then Noah locked the doors.

Now God called again to Noah and said: "It is your turn now, to go into the ark—you and your family, for it will rain very soon. Do not be afraid, for no harm can come to you. And when this great rain is over, I promise you, there will never be so much rain again."

Noah and his wife, and Shem and Ham and Japheth with their wives (eight people in all), went into the ark and closed the doors behind them. The rain began to fall, and it rained and rained and rained, for forty days and forty nights. There never was so much rain, either before or since then; and it was called "The Flood," because it washed away the cities, and the houses, and everything in them.

Every day Noah had looked out of the window to see whether the rain was still falling, but at last, one morning as he looked out, he saw there was no more rain. The ark had been sailing on the water, for there had been so much rain, that the water covered all the ground, and it looked like an ocean.

As the water began to dry up, the ark settled on the top of a mountain, and rested there. Noah opened one of the windows, and sent out a raven, to see if the ground was dry enough for them to leave the ark. But the raven flew back and forth, back and forth and Noah could not tell much about it.

Noah waited seven days, and then sent out a dove. Towards evening he heard a soft "tap-tap-tap" on the window, and when he opened it, there was the little dove, all cold and wet and tired. There was so much water all over the ground, that the little dove found no place to rest. Noah took her into the ark again, and gave her something to eat.

Noah waited seven days more, and sent the dove out again. Towards evening he heard the same "tap-tap-tap" on the window. He opened it, and saw the little dove. And what do you think? This time she carried a little olive leaf in her mouth! And Noah knew that the waters had dried up.

Still he waited seven days more, and when he sent the dove out again, she did not come back. Then Noah

NOAH LEAVING THE ARK.

THE GREAT RAIN

and his sons removed the roof of the ark, and were happy to see the sun again, and the dry land and the green grass.

God spoke to Noah again and said: "Go out of the ark now, you and your wife, and your sons and their wives, and every living thing that is in the ark."

That was a busy time for Noah and the whole family, to get all those animals ready to leave, and it was a great and happy procession that came out of that ark. How glad the birds were to fly up into the branches of the trees! How fast the animals ran into the woods! And the insects crept into the grass and bushes so quickly, that soon nothing was to be seen except Noah and his family.

Noah told his sons that they must build an altar, and bring a sacrifice, to show God that they thanked Him for saving them from drowning. They went into the woods, and looked for good, dry sticks for the altar. The flames and smoke rose up into the air in a beautiful straight line.

As Noah and his sons looked up towards the sky to watch the smoke, do you know what they saw? There up in the sky was the beautiful rainbow, with its seven bright colors: red, yellow, blue, orange, green, violet and indigo.

Then Noah heard the voice of God saying:

"I will bless you and your family, and I promise never to send another flood. There will sometimes be heavy clouds, and there will often be rainstorms, but there will always be the beautiful rainbow in the sky. This will show all the world that I remember what I told Noah. The rainbow will be God's 'Bow of Promise' forever."

IV

THE VISIT OF THE ANGELS

ABRAHAM

Once upon a time, in a country named Mamre, there lived a very good man whose name was Abraham. He owned hundreds and hundreds of acres of land, and had thousands of oxen, and cows, and goats, and sheep. He also had much silver and gold. He kept many servants to do all his work for him, and they all lived in tents. Abraham and his family lived in tents, too, because in that warm country tents were more comfortable than houses.

Abraham loved all the people around him, and he was so kind to everybody that they all loved him. Abraham loved God, and used to pray to Him at night and in the morning. You see, at this time, the people knew much more than they did when Adam and Eve were living, for they had learned about things. So, although they still built altars, and brought sacrifices, they also knew how to pray to God to thank Him for all His goodness.

Abraham was good to every one, and always tried to do things to make people happy and contented. Living in the same house with Abraham was his nephew, whose name was Lot. Lot had lived with his Uncle Abraham for many years, from the time when he was a very little boy. When he grew to be a man, Abraham gave him many sheep and goats and cows and oxen for his very own.

After about a year there were many little baby animals. You cannot guess how much land it took, and how many big fields, covered with grass, they had to have to give enough food to all the animals that belonged to Abraham and to Lot. Of course, where there were so many animals there had to be many men-servants to take care of them out in the fields. These men often quarreled, and made trouble for Abraham and Lot.

One day Abraham said to Lot:

"I do not like all these quarrels between our men. You and I are relations, and we love each other, but our servants quarrel too much. I own all the land around here, and I want you to choose part of it for yourself.

THE VISIT OF THE ANGELS

Then you can take your servants and your cattle away, and that will stop the quarreling."

Abraham and Lot went up on a high hill, and from there looked around upon the beautiful fields and valleys. Then Abraham said:

"All this land is mine, but you can choose any part you like, and I will give it to you for a present. If you want the fields on this side of the hill, take them, and I will keep the others. Or, if you like the fields on the other side better, take those, and I will keep these."

Don't you think Lot's uncle was very kind? It all belonged to Abraham, and he might have said:

"I am going to keep the nicest fields for my cattle, because they are mine, and you can take those way over there." But he would not do anything so selfish, and he let Lot choose for himself.

Lot looked around at the beautiful country. Then he chose the fields that he wanted, and told his men to take all the cattle there. When he came back to Abraham to thank him, and to bid him good-bye, Abraham kissed him, and said:

"Good-bye, Lot. I hope God will take care of you, and I hope you will be happy in your new home."

But although Abraham was a very rich man he was often sad, because he had no children. One day, when he was sitting at the door of his tent, he saw three strange men coming along the road. It was a very warm day, and the men were hot and tired, and their shoes were covered with dust.

Abraham, who was always kind and thoughtful and considerate, called to the men to come into his nice cool tent and rest there. He gave them seats, and then went into the next tent, which was used for a kitchen. His wife, Sarah, was there, and he told her to get some food for the three tired men.

Abraham then filled a bucket with fresh water, took some towels, and went back to his own tent. He knelt down on the floor by the men, and took off their shoes and stockings. He also bathed their feet in the nice cool water, and the men soon felt rested and comfortable. When the food was ready, the men ate it, and enjoyed their dinner.

Late in the afternoon, when it was cool, the three men rose to go. Abraham stood at the door with them to say good-bye. They told Abraham they were not travelers, but angels whom God had sent. The angels

THE ANGELS PROMISE A CHILD TO ABRAHAM

THE VISIT OF THE ANGELS

said God knew that Abraham's only wish was to have children, and they promised that God would give him his wish. Then they went away.

Abraham had two wives, Sarah and Hagar, and, later, two little boys, Ishmael and Isaac. Ishmael was a wild, careless boy. He always wanted to be in the woods or any place outdoors, and he often worried his father. He was not really a bad boy, but he was very mischievous, and did many things that annoyed and bothered people.

You will soon learn how much trouble that made for him and for his mother, Hagar. The other boy, Isaac, was a good little fellow, who liked to stay in the tent with his mother, Sarah, and he loved to listen to the wonderful stories his father told him. Isaac was very obedient, too.

One day Abraham gave a party. Ishmael was quite a big boy, and he knew how to behave well, if he wanted to. But, like many other boys who try to show off when there is company in the house, Ishmael did all sorts of silly things that he thought were smart and funny.

Abraham and Sarah were very much ashamed of him. After the party was over, Sarah told Abraham that Ishmael must be punished. So the next day Abraham told Ishmael that he must go away, and his mother, Hagar, would go with him.

Abraham was sorry to punish Ishmael in this way, but Sarah said she would not keep such a bad boy as Ishmael in the same house as her little Isaac. You see, she was afraid Ishmael would make Isaac just as bad as he was. So they had to go away from his father's house.

They wandered for many days, through valleys and over hills, picking berries to eat, and sleeping in the warm thick grass. At last they came to a desert. It was very hot there, and not a shady place to be seen. Ishmael was so tired and thirsty he did not know what to do. He lay down upon the hot sand and did not move.

His poor mother, Hagar, was very unhappy, for she was afraid her boy would die if he did not soon get a drink of water. She looked all around her, and, to her great joy, saw a little pool of water not far away. After Ishmael had a good drink, and had washed his face and head, he felt better. By the time the sun set, he was strong enough to walk again.

After a very long journey, Hagar and Ishmael found

THE VISIT OF THE ANGELS

a place near the Wilderness of Paran, and they remained there. Ishmael grew up to be a very strong and healthy man, and he became a great hunter and archer. (An archer is a man who can shoot well with bow and arrows.)

V

THE RAM ON THE MOUNTAIN

ISAAC

Do you know what a ram is? It is a very large sheep with strong, curved horns. But before I tell you anything more about that, we must go back to the tents of Abraham, to see what he and little Isaac have been doing. Abraham was a very old man now, but he was just as good to every one as he always had been, and everybody loved and trusted him.

Abraham was the same as a chief, that is, he ruled over the people. But they did not call him a chief, they called him a patriarch. That is a pretty long word for you to remember; but I think you can if you try. Pa-tri-arch. Abraham never went very far from his tent because he was so old, but he always sat by the open door. Every one could see him sitting there, and could come to him when they wanted him to help them.

One day, when he was there by the tent door, he heard a Voice calling:

THE RAM ON THE MOUNTAIN

"Abraham!" and he answered: "Here am I."

"Go up to the land of Moriah," said the Voice again. "Take the boy, Isaac, with you. Go up into the mountain, and offer the boy as a sacrifice."

Don't you think Abraham must have felt very unhappy to think that he had to take his little boy for a sacrifice? Abraham loved God and had always obeyed Him, so he knew he would obey now, even though he felt very sorry to do so.

The next morning Abraham told two of the menservants to gather wood for the sacrifice. When they brought it, Abraham tied a bundle of sticks together, and fastened the bundle upon Isaac's back. He took a large sharp knife, and some dried grass to start the fire, and they left home.

Little Isaac trudged along by his father's side, often singing to himself. He wondered where they were going, and what his father would do. When they had come to the foot of the mountain Abraham told the two men to wait there for him until he returned. The men wondered why they had to stay there, but they obeyed.

As Isaac and his father were climbing up the side of the mountain, Isaac began to ask all kinds of questions, like children always do, but his father only said:

"Wait, my son. You will find out when we reach the top of the mountain."

"Father," said Isaac, "I only want to ask one question more. May I?"

His father nodded his head, and Isaac said:

"I am carrying the wood for the fire, and I see your knife, but where is the sacrifice?"

"God will provide the sacrifice," answered Abraham, but he turned his head away, so Isaac should not see the tears in his eyes.

Isaac asked no more questions, but trotted along very cheerfully with his bundle of wood. When they came to a small open space at the top of the mountain Abraham took the bundle from Isaac's shoulders. The little fellow straightened himself up, and threw back his shoulders, for the bundle was heavy, and it was not a very easy thing to carry up to the top of a mountain.

Abraham found a smooth stone, and Isaac helped lay the sticks evenly and straight. Then Abraham said in a low voice:

"Isaac, my son, God has sent no other sacrifice. I must put you on the altar, for you must be the sacrifice."

THE SACRIFICE OF ISAAC

THE RAM ON THE MOUNTAIN

Isaac was very brave. He did not scream, nor cry, nor beg, but was perfectly still while his father tied him down on the altar. Abraham stooped to pick up the knife. At that instant he heard God's voice calling his name.

"Here am I," answered Abraham, and God said:

"Do not harm the boy. I only wanted to see if you would obey me, and if the boy would obey you. You have both obeyed; but I do not wish such a sacrifice."

As Abraham untied Isaac and lifted him from the altar, he saw a big ram held fast in some bushes by his strong horns. Abraham caught him, and he and Isaac knew God had sent the sacrifice. God spoke again to Abraham and said:

"You were obedient, even when you thought God was not just. You were willing to give your own dear little boy as a sacrifice. Therefore I will reward you forever. I will bless you and all your people, and will give you health and riches and happiness."

Isaac loved his father and mother very dearly, and always tried to please them. He grew up to be a fine young man, and, when his father said it was time for him to marry, he said he was willing.

Abraham had an old servant that he trusted with everything. Abraham spoke to him, and said he must go away and find a good wife for Isaac.

"How can I tell who will be a good wife?" asked the servant.

"You will see many young girls in different places," said Abraham, "and the one who will be very kind to you, she will be the wife for Isaac."

The man got ready to go. He took ten fine camels, and on their backs he loaded many presents for the cousins of Abraham who lived in the nearest town. Abraham had given him these presents to take with him, and they were very handsome presents, because Abraham was such a rich man.

One afternoon, a few days later, the old servant and his camels came to the gates of a city. A large well was near the gate, and many young girls stood around the well. Each one had a jug or a pitcher in her hand, in which to carry the fresh water home. They were laughing and talking, as one after the other filled her pitcher with water, and none of them seemed to notice the man or his camels.

One girl had been watching them, and she saw how

tired and dusty they all looked. She walked over to where the camels were resting on the ground, and the servant said:

"Will you please give me a drink of water out of your pitcher?"

"Yes, indeed," she answered, "and I will draw enough water from the well for all your camels to drink."

She handed her pitcher to the man, and then went back to the well. There was a watering-trough near the well, and the girl filled it with water for the camels. When she had finished drawing the water, the man said:

"Who are you? What is your name? And is there room in your father's house for me?"

You see, he asked those questions to find out if the young girl was as polite as she was kind. And she said:

"I am the daughter of Bethuel. My name is Rebecca and I am sure there is room in my father's house for you, and we have a place for your camels."

The man saw she was sweet and kind and polite, so he was sure she would be a good wife for Isaac. He went home with her, and told her father that Abraham had sent him. He gave her father many presents and asked him to let Rebecca go back with him to be Isaac's wife. The father was willing, and in a few days the man took Rebecca away.

While the faithful servant was away on his errand, Sarah, Isaac's mother, died. Isaac was very grieved and sad. Waiting at home, with his father, he often wondered if the servant would bring a young girl back with him. Every day he walked along the road to the city to look if they were coming. At last, one morning, he saw a train of camels far down the road, and he knew the camels were his father's.

Isaac hurried to meet them and saw Rebecca. She was so sweet and pretty that he loved her even before he spoke to her. The servant told her this young man was Isaac. Isaac was tall and handsome, and Rebecca loved him, too. They all went home to Abraham, who was very happy to see this lovely girl, and in a few days Isaac and Rebecca were married.

VI

THE BROTHERS

ESAU AND JACOB

Isaac and Rebecca had two sons named Esau and Jacob. Esau was a boy who loved animals very much. When he was a little boy he used to play with any animal he could, a cat or a dog or a horse or a rabbit. He did not care what it was, as long as it was an animal, and many times he used to stay out in the woods all day long, and forget about his dinner.

Jacob was a quiet little boy, who always wanted to be around his mother. He did not care for animals, and he never went out with Esau. Sometimes the two boys played together, but not very often. Isaac loved Esau best, but the mother was fonder of Jacob, although she loved Esau, too.

As Esau grew older he became a hunter, and he often brought home the animals he had killed, for the family to eat. Esau knew just how to clean the skins, and how to dry them. Afterwards these skins were used for rugs on the floor, and sometimes he hung them across his back and shoulders, like a coat.

It pleased Isaac to see how much Esau could do, and Esau liked to do things for his father. Esau had learned to cook pretty well, and Isaac always was glad to have Esau cook the fresh meat for him. Being out in the air all the time, Esau's skin was rough and hard, and his face and hands were covered with hair.

Jacob, who stayed in the house so much, had skin as soft as a girl's, and he had no hair on his hands or his face. Isaac could not see very well, for he was old, and nearly blind. When his sons came near him, he used to feel their hands and faces, and could tell who it was, whether it was Esau or Jacob.

One day Isaac told Esau to get some venison, (deer's meat), and cook a nice meal for him. Isaac said: "Get the meat, Esau, and after I have eaten of it, I will give you my blessing."

Do you know what a blessing is? It is a prayer to God to ask Him to bless some person, to care for, and to watch over that person. When any body says: "God bless you," it means God should take care of you.

Esau was very glad to get the venison for his father.

THE BROTHERS

He wanted to please his father, and he wanted his father to give him the blessing. He took his bow and arrows, and he hurried off into the forest as quickly as he could.

While Isaac was talking to Esau, Rebecca stood by the door of her tent, and she heard what Isaac said. It made her cross, because she loved Jacob best, and she wanted Jacob to have the blessing. She stood there thinking about it for a little while, and then went into the tent where Jacob was.

She quickly told Jacob all about it, and then said: "I am going to cook a fine dinner for your father. When it is ready, you shall take it to him, and get his blessing."

"Oh! I cannot do that," said Jacob, "because my father will know I am Jacob. Esau is a hairy man, and I am a smooth man. My father will feel my hands and my face, and he will know I am Jacob."

"Never mind," said his mother, "I will look out for that. You just go and bring in some of the dried goat-skins, and I will make you hairy."

While Jacob was gone, Rebecca cooked some meat just as Isaac liked it most, and made some little cakes. When Jacob came back with the goat skins, she tied them around his shoulders and his head. She also pinned pieces of the skin over his hands. Then she gave him the food for his father.

Jacob really did not want to deceive the poor old man, who was so nearly blind, but his mother said he must do as she told him. She said Esau was so wild, he would not really care for the blessing, and she wanted Jacob to have it. Jacob took the tray with the dinner on it, and went to his father. When Isaac heard footsteps outside, he asked:

"Is it you, my son Esau? How did you get back here so soon?" And Jacob said:

"I found a deer near here, and you know, father, it does not take very long to cook venison."

"Come close to me, my son," said Isaac. "I want to know if you are Esau;" and when he felt the hairy hands and neck, he said:

"Your hands feel like Esau's, but your voice is Jacob's."

The father took the food, and after he finished eating, he said: "Come nearer to me, my son, and I will bless you. I am old, and I cannot live much longer, but I want to bless you before I die."

ISAAC GIVES JACOB HIS BLESSING

THE BROTHERS

Jacob knelt down at his father's side, and bowed his head. Isaac placed his two hands on his son's head, and gave him the same blessing that God had given to Abraham long before, and which God had promised to his children and children's children.

Isaac told Jacob he would, some day, be the father of many sons and of a great nation of people. Then he asked God to bless Jacob with health and wisdom and wealth; and Isaac kissed him on his head. Jacob rose from his knees, and stood by his father. He thanked his father and then went to tell his mother.

While Jacob was in the tent with his father, Esau had come back with a large deer he had shot. He cut a slice of meat from the tenderest part of the deer, and prepared it with a nice sauce that his father liked. When it was ready, he carried the dish into his father's tent, and called out cheerily:

"Here I am, father, and here is some fine venison I have brought you."

"Who are you?" asked poor old Isaac in a trembling voice. "Who are you? I cannot see. Come nearer."

Esau knelt down before his father, very close to him, and said: "Don't you know me, father? I am Esau, and here is the meat you wished for. Eat it, I beg of you, and then give me your blessing."

Isaac was very sad when he heard his son beg for the blessing, and he said slowly:

"Oh, my son Esau, I have given the blessing to your brother Jacob. He brought me food, and I ate it. I thought he was you, and I blessed him and his children forever."

"But, father," cried Esau, "have you only one blessing to give? Can you not bless me, too?"

Then Isaac rose from his chair, and laying his hand on Esau's head, answered:

"The blessing that should have been yours, I gave to Jacob, and it can never be taken away from him. All I can say to you is, that you will always be a good hunter, and you will be a rich man and a great man." Esau then left his father's tent, but he was very angry at Jacob.

Rebecca had heard all that Isaac said to Esau, and she told Jacob he must go away for awhile, until Esau forgot all about the blessing; and then Jacob could come back again. So Jacob went, but he was not very happy when he thought of what had happened. He knew how

THE BROTHERS

wrong it was to deceive his kind father, and to take away the blessing from his brother. And he was very sorry he had been so wicked.

One night he lay down to sleep in a field. He had no covering and no pillow, so he laid his head on a big flat stone. He slept, and had a queer dream. He dreamed he saw a ladder that reached way up to the sky, and that many angels were climbing up and down the ladder. And he dreamed that God stood on the top of the ladder. And he heard God say to him: "Jacob, I will bless you with many blessings."

When Jacob woke the next morning, he remembered his beautiful dream, and he thought he had been in heaven with God. Jacob said the field was holy ground. He took the stone that had been his pillow, stood it up on the spot where he dreamed he had seen the ladder, and called the place "Beth-el," which means "God's House."

Then he knelt down by the stone, and prayed to God. He said he was very sorry for what he had done to his father and his brother, and he asked God to forgive him for the wrong he had done. He promised God he would always be a good man. And he kept his word.

Long afterward Jacob and Esau met again. They talked together a long while, they gave each other many handsome presents, and they became good friends.

VII

THE DREAMER

JOSEPH

Jacob went to a beautiful land called Canaan, and stayed there. He married, and had thirteen children, twelve boys and one girl. He owned much land and cattle, and people said he was a very rich man. Jacob loved all his children, but he loved Joseph more than the others, because Joseph was such a gentle and kind boy.

The brothers of Joseph did not like him very much; I suppose because the father loved him most. Joseph liked to lie under the trees, on the nice soft grass, and liked to listen to the singing of the birds. He loved to watch the pretty, white clouds floating in the air nearly up to the sky, and he would keep very quiet, and dream away the time.

His brothers, just to tease him, called him the dreamer. One day, Jacob gave Joseph a fine, new coat. That made his brothers angry, for they thought Joseph did not need another coat. The brothers used to go away from home every morning to take the cattle to the fields.

Once Jacob called Joseph, and said: "Go and find your brothers. I told them to go to the East fields. See if they are there, and what they are doing, and come back soon to tell me."

Joseph went to look for them, but when he came to the East fields, no one was there except an old man. Joseph asked him whether he had seen his brothers. The old man said they had not been near the East fields at all, but he had seen them go way over to the West fields. Joseph hurried to the other fields.

One of the brothers saw him coming, and said to the others: "Here comes that dreamer Joseph, and I wonder what he wants. When he goes back home, he will tell our father we did not go to the East fields, and then our father will not trust us any more. Let us kill Joseph, and tell father a wild beast rushed out of the forest, and ate the boy."

"Oh no," said Reuben, the oldest brother. "Don't let us do that. That would be wicked and cruel. Let us put him into that deep pit over there, and he cannot get out."

THE DREAMER

Do you know why Reuben said this? Because he did not want his little brother to be hurt, and because he had made up his mind that after the brothers went home, he would come back alone, and take Joseph out of the pit. Then Reuben went away to look for some sheep that had run off.

When Joseph came, the brothers caught hold of him and took off his new coat. They let him down into the pit, and left him there. After they had climbed up the side of the pit, they killed a goat and dipped Joseph's coat in the blood. They did this, so that they could show it to their father, and tell him a wild beast had killed Joseph.

While they were busy with the coat, they noticed a company of men and a train of camels coming along the road. One of the brothers said: "These men are strangers to us. This is the road that goes into Egypt. If they are going into Egypt, let us ask them to buy Joseph and take him along with them. That will be a good way to get rid of him altogether."

When the men came near, the brothers asked the leader if they would like to buy a young boy who could work for them, and they said yes. They went down into the pit with ropes and pulled Joseph out. The leader paid them twenty pieces of silver, and took Joseph with him.

Towards evening, after the brothers had gone home with their flocks, Reuben went down into the pit to get his brother Joseph, but he was not there. Reuben cried and sobbed, and ran after his brothers.

"Oh, where is my brother Joseph?" he cried. "I could not find him in the pit. What did you do with him?"

They showed Reuben the bloody coat, and said they were taking it home to show their father what had happened.

As soon as Jacob saw them, he said: "Where is my boy—my Joseph? I sent him to the fields after you. Tell me, where is my boy?"

After they had showed him the coat, poor Jacob said: "This is his coat; and some wild animal must have jumped on him and killed my Joseph."

He cried and cried, and Reuben tried to comfort him. But he would not be comforted, and he said he would always mourn for his son.

Joseph was taken to Egypt and a man, whose name

JOSEPH SOLD BY HIS BROTHERS

THE DREAMER

was Potiphar, bought him from the men who had him.

Joseph had a good sweet face and a gentle manner and kind ways, and Potiphar was very fond of him. He was good to Joseph, for he saw how hard Joseph tried to please everybody. Once when Potiphar had to go into the country to attend to some business, he told Joseph to do many things while he was gone.

Potiphar had a wife, who often told Joseph to do things for her, and he always did them when he could. But one day, she told him to do a very foolish thing. Joseph knew it would be wrong if he did it, so he told her he could not. This made her very angry, and when Potiphar came home she told him that Joseph would not obey her, and that he should put Joseph in prison. And Potiphar did what his wife told him.

But God had always watched over Joseph. God knew that Joseph had done what was right and honorable, so, even in the dark prison, God watched over him, too. All the men belonging to the prison were kind to Joseph, and before long, they took him out of the dark cell where he was. They let Joseph help them in their work, and he made friends with every one.

Just about this time, the butler who served the king,

did something wrong, and was put into the prison where Joseph was. The butler remained in prison many months. One morning as Joseph was going around doing his work, he noticed how sad the butler looked.

Joseph, who was always kind to everyone, asked what it was that worried the butler. The butler said he had dreamed a queer dream, and he asked Joseph if he could tell him what the dream meant. Joseph told him to tell the dream, and maybe he could tell him the meaning.

The butler said: "I dreamed I saw a grape-vine with three branches on it. I saw the green leaves and the ripe purple grapes. I held the cup of King Pharaoh in my hand. I pressed the juice of the grapes into the cup, and then I handed it to the king to drink."

"I can easily tell you what that dream means," said Joseph. "The three branches are three days, and in three days from now, King Pharaoh will send for you to leave this prison. The king will set you free, and you will be his butler again, and you will hand him his cup of wine like you always did."

The butler was very happy, and said to Joseph: "I thank you for telling me what my dream means. Is there anything I can do for you after I leave this prison?"

"Yes," answered Joseph. "When you are back in the king's palace, will you ask King Pharaoh to set me free? I never did any wrong to anybody, and I do not belong in Egypt at all."

Everything happened just as Joseph said. Three days later was the king's birthday, and he made a feast for all his servants. He sent to prison for the butler, and let him work in the palace just as he used to do. But the butler forgot all about poor Joseph in prison, and he did not tell the king anything about what was going on there.

VIII

THE GOVERNOR OF EGYPT

JOSEPH

Two years after Joseph was put in prison, King Pharaoh had a strange dream. The king dreamed he stood by the side of a river. He saw seven cows come up out of the water to eat the grass that was growing on the banks of the river. These cows were fat and healthy cows, and while they were eating the grass, seven other cows came up out of the water; but these cows were thin and sick. For a minute, the sick cows looked at the well ones. Then the thin and sick cows ate up the fat and healthy ones.

Pharaoh woke up, and wondered what the dream meant. While he was thinking about it, he fell asleep again, and had another dream. This time, the king dreamed he was standing by a field of corn, and on a tall stalk, he saw seven ears of corn. They were large ears full of corn. But just below them, on the same stalk, there were seven very thin ears with very little

THE GOVERNOR OF EGYPT

corn on them. While the king was looking at them, the seven thin ears swallowed the seven full ears. Then the king woke up; and he was very much worried by the dreams.

In those times, there were wise men in Egypt who sometimes understood dreams, and could tell what the dreams meant. King Pharaoh sent his servants to bring all the wise men to the palace, so that he could tell them his dreams. They came very quickly, but none of them knew what the dreams meant.

Then the butler remembered Joseph, and said to Pharaoh: "Great king, I am ashamed to say that I forgot something, but I will tell you now. When I was in prison long ago, a young man was there who was very kind to all the prisoners. I know he can tell the meaning of dreams."

The king sent to the prison for Joseph. But before Joseph went to the palace he shaved himself. Then he asked for clean clothes, which they gave him. When Joseph was brought to the king, King Pharaoh said: "My servants say that you understand dreams, and can tell what any dream means. Is this true?"

Joseph answered in a low tone: "I cannot always do

that. Sometimes God puts the thoughts in my mind. If you tell me your dreams, perhaps God will help me."

Pharaoh told his two dreams, and Joseph listened quietly. Then he said: "These two dreams are really only one dream, because they both mean the same thing. God sent these dreams to you, so that you may know what will soon happen in your land."

Joseph explained the dreams in this way: "The seven fat cows and the seven full ears of corn mean seven years of plenty; plenty of cattle, plenty of flocks and herds, plenty of grain, plenty of water, plenty of everything. The seven thin cows and the thin ears of corn mean seven years of famine, when there will be very little to eat. After the seven good years of plenty, there will be seven years when the grain will not grow. The animals will have very little to eat, and many will die, and the people will not have much food either."

Pharaoh did not speak for a few minutes, then he said: "I think I understand the dreams now. Tell me, Joseph, do you know what I can do to stop the bad years from coming? What can I do, so that my people will have enough to eat, and what can be done to get food for the cattle and sheep?"

THE GOVERNOR OF EGYPT

"God sent you these dreams," said Joseph, "so you can be ready when the bad years of famine come. First of all, you must choose a good and wise man to be the Governor of Egypt. Then you must let the people all know that you trust this man. And the people must obey the governor and do all he says."

"Yes," said the king, "and I know a man who will make a good governor."

"Then," said Joseph, "this is what the governor must do. He must order the men in every city in Egypt to build store-houses,—places to pack away grain and other food. The seven years of plenty will begin now, so there is time enough to do everything. After the store-houses are built, the people must carry food there. The governor must lock up the store-houses so that no one can touch the food, for it must be saved, and when the seven bad years of famine come, there will be enough to eat in Egypt."

King Pharaoh had listened to all Joseph said, and he could tell that Joseph was a very wise man. So he said:

"Joseph, I will make you the governor of Egypt, and you can order everything done just as you think best."

The king took a beautiful gold ring from his own finger and gave it to Joseph. He put a long gold chain around Joseph's neck and sent for fine new clothes for Joseph to wear.

So you see what happened to Joseph. Because he had always been so kind to everyone, everyone loved him. Because he loved God and trusted in Him, the boy who had been sold by his brothers to be a servant, became the governor of the great land of Egypt.

During the next seven years, the years of plenty in Egypt, Joseph was very busy. He watched the workmen build the great store-houses and he made all the farmers bring a certain amount of grain to put into them. So, when the good years had passed away, there was enough food in the many store-houses in Egypt to last for the seven bad years that were coming.

But in the other lands around Egypt, no one had tried to save up, and they all had to go to Joseph, the governor of Egypt, to buy what they needed. Down in the land of Canaan where Jacob and his family lived, there was hardly any food for the cattle to eat.

Jacob told his sons they must go to Egypt to buy corn. They did not want to go. Do you know why? Just be-

THE GOVERNOR OF EGYPT

cause they remembered how they had sold their brother to men who took him to Egypt. They were afraid they would meet Joseph and they thought Joseph would do them some harm. But they did not know that Joseph was the governor of Egypt.

Jacob said they must go, and gave them money to buy corn. Each one of the brothers took a big bag to carry back the corn. When they came to Egypt, they went to the store-house where Joseph was selling grain. They saw Joseph standing there, and bowed down to him because he was the governor. They did not know he was their brother, for when they sold him he was a boy, and now he was a man.

It was thirteen years since Joseph was sold, but as soon as he saw his brothers, he knew them again. He made believe he did not know them, and spoke very roughly to them. He said: "What do all you men want here?"

"We came from the land of Canaan to buy corn," answered the brothers.

"I do not think so," said Joseph. "I think you are spies, and that you came here to see what is going on in Egypt."

"No, great governor," said Reuben, "we are not spies. We are brothers, and we came to buy corn. We do not want to know what is going on in Egypt."

They then told Joseph that there were twelve brothers in their family, but now, one was dead. (You see, they thought Joseph was dead.) Reuben said their youngest brother was at home. When Joseph said they must bring their youngest brother to see him, Reuben said: "Our father will not let him come. He loves our brother, Benjamin, so much, that he always wants him at home."

"Tell your father," said Joseph, "that Benjamin must come. And I will keep one of you here until he does come."

He pointed to one of the brothers and two officers took him away. Joseph ordered his servants to fill the bags with corn, and sent his brothers to bring Benjamin back. The brothers, all except the one Joseph had kept with him, went home. They were afraid to tell their father that the governor of Egypt wished to see Benjamin, but they had to.

"No, no," said the father. "I cannot let my Benjamin go to Egypt. Many years ago, I sent Joseph out

THE GOVERNOR OF EGYPT

into the fields to you, and he never came back. If anything should happen to Benjamin, so that he cannot come back to me, I would die of sorrow."

But after sometime, when all the corn was used up, Reuben told his father they must have more food for the cattle. He said Egypt was the only place where they could buy corn. He begged so long for Benjamin to go with them, that at last, the father consented.

When they came to Egypt, to the governor's house Joseph said: "How is your father? I hope he is well."

"Yes," said Reuben, "he is quite well."

"Is this your brother, Benjamin?" asked Joseph, as he looked at the pretty boy standing by Reuben.

"This is our brother, Benjamin," said Reuben, "and he is our father's darling."

Joseph did not answer, but rushed out of the room. He was so glad to see his little brother, that he began to cry, and he did not want any one to see him cry. When Joseph came back into the room, he sent all the servants away. Then he said to his brothers: "It is true, I am the governor of Egypt, but I am also your brother, Joseph, the boy you sold so many years ago."

The brothers all looked so scared, that Joseph said

quickly: "You need not be afraid, I will not harm you, for I forgave you long ago. That was God's way to make me a great man, and now I am the greatest man in Egypt, except the king. I am rich and I can do whatever I like, and I want all of you to come here to live. Now go home and bring our father to me."

Joseph gave them corn, and sent them away. They went back to Canaan and told their father, Jacob, all that had happened. When they said Joseph was alive, and was the good, wise governor, Jacob folded his hands in prayer to God, and thanked Him for His goodness.

Reuben said Joseph wanted the whole family to come to Egypt and stay there. That he wanted them to bring all their cattle and flocks and herds and Joseph would give them all the land they needed. So one day, they all started from Canaan to go to Egypt.

It was just like a parade. There was old father Jacob and his ten sons—for Joseph and Benjamin were in Egypt. Then there were all the wives and children and grandchildren, and the servants and the flocks and herds. The older people rode in wagons that Joseph had sent from Egypt, the children rode on camels, and the strong men walked.

JOSEPH MAKES HIMSELF KNOWN TO HIS BROTHERS

THE GOVERNOR OF EGYPT

Pharaoh was a good king, and he loved Joseph. He was very glad that Joseph's family was coming to Egypt, and he told Joseph to choose the best land there was for his father and brothers. Just before they all reached the city where Joseph lived, they saw Joseph coming to meet them in his chariot.

Jacob and Joseph were very, very glad to see each other again, as you can imagine, and Jacob thanked God for giving him such happiness. They all found homes near Joseph's palace, and Joseph was always the good true son and brother to them, and he remained the good and wise governor all his life.

IX

THE BABY IN THE BASKET

MOSES

Many years after Joseph's death, there was another king in Egypt whose name was Pharaoh, too. But this Pharaoh was a rough and cruel man and a bad king, while the other Pharaoh, who lived when Joseph was the governor, was a kind man and a good king.

During these years many children were born, and grew up, and got married, and they had children; and when this Pharaoh was made king, there were thousands and thousands of Hebrews in the land. The people of Egypt called the Hebrews, Israelites, and I will tell you why. After old father Jacob had twelve sons, God said his name should be Israel, and that all his people should be called Israelites.

When these Israelites first came into Egypt, they were very happy, because King Pharaoh, Joseph's friend, was very good to them. But the new king was very cruel. He said that they must work for him, and be his slaves.

THE BABY IN THE BASKET

Slaves are people who have to work from morning until night every day, and who never get any money for their work. The masters send food to them, give them ugly little cabins to live in, and give them poor clothes to wear. And that is all they have.

One day King Pharaoh said: "There are too many Israelites in Egypt, and we must do something to get rid of them. I will make a new law. It is that every baby boy that is born to these people must be killed right away." Don't you think he was a cruel king? And just think how unhappy that law made those poor people—to have to kill their dear little baby boys!

There was one woman who said she would not have her baby killed, so she hid him for three months. Then she was afraid that some of the king's soldiers would find him. So she made a basket of bulrushes, which is a thick, heavy grass that grows along the edges of a lake or a river. She made it in the shape of a little boat, and covered it with tar, so the water could not get inside. She put some soft cotton in the bottom of the little boat, and laid her little boy on the cotton. She then set the basket in the weeds that were down by the river, and told her daughter Miriam to watch it. The girl hid behind some trees to see what would happen to the baby. Soon she saw the lovely princess, the daughter of King Pharaoh, coming down to the bank of the river.

The princess was walking slowly along with some of her maidens when she saw the little basket, and she sent one of the girls to bring it to her. When she lifted off the cover, she saw that sweet little baby boy. He looked at her with his big black eyes, and smiled up into her face. The princess said: "What a darling baby! He must belong to some Israelite woman, and I know she put him in this basket to save his life. He is too sweet to die, and I will take him home with me to keep for my very own." Just then she saw Miriam. She motioned for her to come near, and said: "I have just taken this little boy out of the water. I will keep him for my own and he shall live with me in the palace. Can you find some woman to be his nurse?"

You can imagine how glad Miriam was, and she told the princess she would bring a nurse to the palace in a few minutes. She ran home as fast as she could, and told her mother to go to the palace at once. The mother was very happy, for now she could stay with her own

THE BABY BOY MOSES HIDDEN
IN THE BULRUSHES

THE BABY IN THE BASKET

little baby. She went quickly to the palace, and the princess said: "I want you to nurse this little boy. I just found him out in the river, and I have named him Moses. Moses means 'taken out of the water,' and I took the child out of the water. Now be sure to take good care of the little fellow."

You may be sure that the nurse, who was his own mother, took good care of the little Moses and was very kind to him. Moses grew up to be a fine boy, and he loved the princess and his mother-nurse very dearly. When he was old enough, the princess got good teachers for him, and he learned everything that a prince should know. He loved to study, and to learn about things, and when he grew to be a man, he was very wise.

All the people of Egypt, the Egyptians and the Israelites, all loved Moses very much. He was gentle and kind to everyone, and he was very good to animals. But, although Moses lived in the king's palace, and was treated like a prince by everybody, and although he had everything he wished for, he was always sad. I wonder if you can guess why.

He knew he was an Israelite and he was sad because

he had everything to make him comfortable and happy, and his people had nothing at all but hard work. You see, his mother had told him many stories when he was little. They were all about his own people, and he loved them. It made him sad that he could not do anything for them to help them in some way.

One day he went out for a walk. He passed a place where a number of men were building a new house. The workmen were all Israelites and the man who watched them at work was an Egyptian. One of the Israelites was carrying a heavy load of bricks. He stumbled over a loose board in the floor and the bricks fell down. The Egyptian took his whip and struck the poor Israelite. This made Moses so angry that he struck the Egyptian.

Of course, it was very wrong for Moses to do that, but I suppose he could not help it when he saw how rough the man was and how cruel, too. Afterwards Moses thought how foolish he had been, for he could not go around and strike every Egyptian who was cruel to an Israelite. So he thought that just now the best thing he could do would be to go away from Egypt till he could find some way to help his people.

THE BABY IN THE BASKET

He went far away into the country and stopped at a farm house. He asked the farmer if he could give him some work to do on the farm. Just think of that! Why, he might have remained in the palace and be a prince and have anything he wanted there! But Moses said as long as the other Israelites had to work, he would work, too. So he began by taking care of sheep.

One evening, after he had brought the sheep home and counted them to see if all were there, he noticed that one little lamb was gone. Moses was cold and tired and hungry, but he did not mind that at all, when he thought of the little lamb out all alone on the hillside. He hurried back to the hills where the sheep had been all day, to look for the lamb.

Moses could not see it anywhere for it was nearly dark, but he heard a soft, low "baa-baa." He knew the little lamb must be close by. He looked around and there it was, lying on the ground under a bush, all tired out and shivering with cold. Moses took it in his arms, wrapped his own coat around it, and, although he was so tired himself, he carried that heavy little lamb all the way home. And then he fed it before he had his own supper.

One day, when Moses was walking alone, he saw a bush that looked as if it were on fire. He walked nearer to it, and saw that though there was a big flame around it, the bush did not burn out. And he heard a Voice speaking from out of the bush, and he knew it was the Voice of God. And the Voice said to him that just as the bush was burning and was not destroyed so would the people of Moses never be destroyed. And Moses took off his sandals and bowed his head in prayer, for he knew he was standing on holy ground.

Moses had a brother, Aaron, who was also a very good man. Moses and Aaron often spoke to each other about the hard work their people had to do. They tried to think of some way to set them free and take them away from Egypt. They both prayed God to help them, or tell them what to do.

At last, one day God spoke to Moses and said: "Go back to Egypt and take your brother Aaron with you. Ask Pharaoh to let your people go into the desert, so they can bring sacrifices to God. If the king does not let the people go, tell him God will punish him."

When Moses and Aaron came to the king, and told him what God had said, Pharaoh answered: "I do

THE BABY IN THE BASKET

not believe a word you say. Your God will not punish such a great king as I am, and I will not let your people go."

Then God sent the punishments, one after the other, till Pharaoh let the people go. He sent the "Ten Plagues" upon the land of Egypt. (A plague is something which gives us pain or worry or unhappiness.)

This was the first plague. All the water was changed into blood. In the rivers and lakes and fountains, and even in the glasses and pitchers, all over, wherever there was any water, it turned into blood. No one had any water to drink, and everybody was afraid. The king was frightened, as well as the people, and he sent for Moses and said: "If your God will make the water clean again I will let your people go."

Moses prayed to God to change the blood back to water again, and God did so. But when Pharaoh saw that the water was clean, he changed his mind and would not let the people go. Then God sent the second plague.

Frogs came. They came from the woods and from the rivers and from the grass. Millions of frogs came and they hopped everywhere. Into houses and pantries, into bureau drawers and wardrobes, upon tables and chairs and even in the beds, there was nothing but frogs.

Then Pharaoh sent for Moses again. He told him if the frogs were taken away he would let the people go. Moses prayed to God to remove the frogs, and soon they all hopped back to the places from which they came. But when they were all gone, the king said he would not let the people go.

Then the third plague was sent. Ugly bugs came. They crawled over everything, and bit everybody. But still the king would not let the people go.

The fourth plague was flies. There were thousands and thousands of flies everywhere.

The fifth plague was a sickness among all the cattle. They were so sick that many died.

The sixth plague was boils, great big ugly sores. All the Egyptians got them all over their bodies, and the boils hurt them badly.

The seventh plague was a great hail-storm. The hail fell so fast and in such big lumps, that the fruit on the trees and the grains in the fields were destroyed.

The eighth plague was locusts. Locusts are insects

THE BABY IN THE BASKET

something like grasshoppers, and the locusts ate everything that was left after the hail-storm.

The ninth plague was darkness. Even in the day time, it was as dark as in the middle of the night, and there was no sun, nor moon, nor stars, to give any light.

During this time, always after each plague came, Pharaoh sent for Moses, and told him the same thing over and over again. He said if God took away the plague, he would let the people go. Then each time after the plague was taken away, Pharaoh changed his mind and would not let the people go.

After the ninth plague, God said to Moses: "I will send one more plague upon Pharaoh and the whole land of Egypt. After that, he will surely let you go."

God told Moses that in the middle of the next night, the oldest or first-born child in every Egyptian family would die—not only the first-born of every family, but the first-born of all the cattle too. God promised that nothing would happen to the Israelites, because God loved them more than the Egyptians.

When God told Moses what he must do to save the Israelites, Moses sent men around to all the people. He told them to go from one house to another wherever an Israelite lived, and told them to say this: "Take as many lambs as you need, and kill them. Then take a little bunch of hyssop (a small plant that grows in Egypt), and dip the leaves in the lamb's blood. Sprinkle this blood on the side of each door of an Israelite's house. After that is done, let every one go inside of the houses, and stay there. No one must go out again until morning comes." And everything was done just as Moses wanted, just as God had ordered it.

Then God spoke to Moses again. He said: "See to it that the people obey me and stay inside their houses tonight. For tonight, I, your God, will send the Angel of Death into every house in Egypt, except those houses where the blood was sprinkled on the doorposts. The Angel of Death will pass over those houses, and no one who is in them will be harmed. For all the years to come, let the children of Israel remember the Passover, and thank God that the Angel of Death did pass over those houses in Egypt."

And that night, at midnight, there was much weeping in Egypt, for in every house and in every barn, and in every field, some one was dead. But in the houses of the Israelites all was well.

THE BABY IN THE BASKET

In that same night, Pharaoh called Moses and Aaron to the palace, and said to them: "Go! go! you and your people. Take your flocks and your herds with you and go! I never want to see any of you again."

Moses gave the order, and the people packed their things very quickly, for they were so poor, they did not have much to pack. Many of them had some dough ready to make bread, but there was no time to bake it, so the women took it as it was. And when they were hungry, they made flat crackers out of the dough which they had brought with them. These crackers are called "matzoh," and thousands of Jews, all over the world, eat them each year at Passover time, instead of bread.

At last, every one was ready to start. The Egyptians were so glad the Israelites were going away, and so glad that the God of Israel had stopped the plagues, that they gave them many presents of gold and silver.

Passover is to the Jews what the Fourth of July is to Americans. It is the day that celebrates the independence of the Jews, just as the Fourth of July celebrates the independence of America. Passover freed the Jews from the King of Egypt, and the Fourth of July freed the Americans from the King of England.

X

THE GREAT LEADER

MOSES

Soon after the people of Israel left Egypt, they chose Moses to be their captain and leader. They said if he would lead the way, they would follow him. Moses prayed God to give him a sign where to lead them, and God said to him: "I will put a pillar of cloud in the sky. Then I will send a wind to blow the cloud in the way I want it to go, and you must follow the cloud. At daytime, it will be a dark pillar of cloud, and at night, it will be a bright column of fire. In that way, you can all see it by night as well as by day."

Moses looked up towards the sky, and there was the pillar of cloud. All day long they followed it, and when night came, the cloud changed to a bright pillar of fire. When it was time to rest, the cloud stood still and did not move at all. Then the people rested.

After the Israelites had left Egypt, Pharaoh began to think how stupid he had been to let them go. These

THE GREAT LEADER

people had done all the hardest work, and now Pharaoh wanted them back. He commanded his soldiers to get ready to follow them, and bring his chariots. (A chariot is a kind of carriage.)

Pharaoh had six hundred chariots, and thousands and thousands of soldiers, and they all hurried to catch the Israelites. These poor people were resting near a body of water called the Red Sea, when they saw Pharaoh's army coming. They were frightened. They told Moses it was all his fault for taking them away from Egypt, and they said they would all be killed.

"Do not be afraid," said Moses. "God has helped us so far, and He will still take care of us. You need only wait a little while, and you will find out that the Egyptians will never bother us any more."

God made a very strong east wind to blow over the sea. This wind swept the waters far to the sides, and made a path right through the middle of the sea, and Moses led them across the Red Sea just as if it were dry land.

When Pharaoh saw this, he said to his soldiers: "Forward, march! Follow quickly while the water is gone."

But God was taking care of His people, and He stopped the wind from blowing, just when the Egyptians started to cross the sea. All the water flowed back again to the middle of the sea, and drowned the wicked king and the soldiers who had been so cruel to the Israelites. Then the people believed that God was taking care of them, and they trusted Moses again.

And now they began their long journey through the desert, where they followed the pillar of cloud by day and the pillar of fire by night. It did not take very long, before the people had eaten all the food they brought with them from Egypt. They put all the blame on Moses again, and said it was his fault they had nothing to eat.

Moses prayed to God again, and God said: "Tell your people I will send them enough to eat. Tell them I will send them Manna." (Manna is a kind of seed or berry that grows in warm countries, and is very good to eat. It is white and sweet, and it tastes like cake.)

God said: "Every morning I will send a rain of Manna, and the people shall pick it up from the ground. They must take only enough for one day's food, and must not save any for the next day. On the sixth day,

MOSES PRESENTING THE TEN COMMANDMENTS
TO THE PEOPLE OF ISRAEL

THE GREAT LEADER

they must pick up enough for two days, because there will be no Manna on the seventh day, for the seventh day is the Sabbath."

Most of the people obeyed Moses, and when the Manna fell to the ground, they took only what they needed for one day. But some of them were very greedy, just as children sometimes are. They took more than they could eat and tried to save it. And what do you think happened? The Manna turned black, and smelled so bad, they were glad to throw it away.

But on the sixth day they gathered enough for two days, because no Manna would be sent on the Sabbath. That Manna did not turn bad, and the people were very careful afterwards, not to take too much Manna on the week-days. So, for awhile they were contented. Then, one day, they found fault with Moses again, and said: "Here we are, traveling around in this desert, with nothing to eat but Manna, and now we cannot even find water to drink. It is all your fault for taking us away from Egypt." Moses prayed God to show him where he could find water.

God told Moses to go back where he would see a large rock near their camp, and told him to strike the rock with his staff and water would flow from it. Moses did as God told him, and a stream of water flowed out of the rock. So the people had all the water they needed.

Moses was very patient with the people, although they gave him trouble all the time. He governed them as well as he could, but they acted like a crowd of naughty children. Moses often went away by himself to pray to God to help him, and once he asked God to give him some rules or laws, which the people would have to obey

And God said that Moses was right. "You need laws to govern the people and I will make the laws. These people are like little children, and always want something they cannot have. They must live here in the desert for many years, until they get some sense." Then God spoke again: "There will come a day when I, your God, will lead you out of this desert into the Promised Land. That is the land I promised to Abraham, Isaac, and Jacob, a land where everything grows and where all the people will be happy. But not yet. You cannot go there until the people are fit to go."

Moses returned to the camp, gave the charge of the people to Aaron, and then went up the mountain to

THE GREAT LEADER

pray. He stayed there a long time, praying earnestly to God for the good of the people, and then God said: "Go back to the camp now. Tell the people to wash their clothes, to clean their tents, and to wash themselves. When everything is perfectly clean, tell your people to pray to God. In three days I, the Lord God, will speak to them from the top of Mount Sinai."

On the morning of the third day, the people saw a thick black cloud upon the mountain. They heard the sound of a trumpet coming from the top of the mountain, and they were afraid. The trumpet call grew louder and louder, and the cloud grew thicker and blacker. It looked like heavy smoke, and the top of Mount Sinai seemed all on fire.

Moses prayed out loud now and asked if God was on the mountain top, and a Voice answered :"I am the Lord, thy God, who brought thee out of the land of Egypt, out of the house of bondage."

Then the Voice spoke these words:

1. THOU SHALT HAVE NO OTHER GOD BUT ME.
2. THOU SHALT NOT MAKE ANY IMAGE OF GOD.
3. THOU SHALT NOT TAKE THE NAME OF GOD IN VAIN.

4. REMEMBER THE SABBATH DAY TO KEEP IT HOLY.
5. HONOR THY FATHER AND THY MOTHER.
6. THOU SHALT NOT KILL.
7. THOU SHALT NOT DO ANY WRONG ACT.
8. THOU SHALT NOT STEAL.
9. THOU SHALT NOT LIE ("bear false witness").
10. THOU SHALT NOT COVET ("covet" is to want other people's things).

The Voice of God,—the thunder and lightning,—the smoke and fire on Mount Sinai,— the loud tones of the trumpet—all these things frightened the people very, very much. They trembled and moved far back away from the mountain, and they cried out to Moses: "After this, you speak to God alone. We beg you to do this, and then tell us what He has said. But do not let God speak to us again for we are afraid of Him."

"You need not be afraid of God," said Moses, "for God loves you all. He wanted to show you how great He is; and He wanted you to be good people, and obey the Ten Commandments that He gave you this day from Mount Sinai."

THE GREAT LEADER

The commandments were written on two stone tablets, and they were very dear to all the people. They called them the "Holy Law" because they were given by God, and they wanted a safe place to keep them. Moses let them make a little house just for the Law. They called it an ark, for it kept the Holy Law just as safe as that big ark kept Noah so long before.

But it was a very different kind of an ark. It was made of the finest kind of wood, and had ornaments on it of real gold and silver. Instead of a door, it had a heavy velvet curtain all trimmed with gold. The curtain hung on large gold rings, and could be moved from side to side. So you see, it was not very much like Noah's ark, was it?

The people of Israel had many troubles in after years. They had many wars with other people, and they wandered from place to place as time passed on, but wherever they went, they carried the ark with them. Sometimes the men would take turns in carrying it, and sometimes it was placed in a small wagon that the men pushed or pulled along. But it was always with them. They said the Holy Law was the most precious thing they had.

Moses himself made many laws to govern the people, and they became orderly, good, and were willing to work. For forty years they lived in the desert, when one day, Moses heard the Voice of God calling him again. God said: "Go to the top of Mount Neboh, and I will show you the land I promised to the Israelites."

Then Moses sent for Joshua who was a very good man. Moses knew the people loved Joshua, so Moses made him the new leader. Moses was a very old man by this time, and he knew he would die soon, even before the people could go into the Promised Land. He saw the beautiful land from the mountain top, and then came back to his people.

Moses called them together to talk to them once more before he said good-bye. He spoke very kindly to them, and told them that Joshua would be the next leader, and, would take them into the Promised Land. He said he was too old and too tired to do anything more for them, and he blessed all the people, and said good-bye.

Moses took his staff, and went up the side of Mount Neboh for the last time. God caused a heavy cloud to cover the whole mountain. Moses laid down to rest and fell into a deep sleep. He never woke again, for God had called him home.

When the people saw that Moses did not come back, they knew he must be dead, and they sobbed and cried, to think they would never see him again. They had loved Moses dearly, because he had always been kind and just and patient. There never was any man, either before or since that time, who was greater than Moses.

XI

THE WOMAN JUDGE

DEBORAH

Our stories have been only about boys and men, but there were many good and wise women in those days, and the Bible tells some pretty stories about them, too. And the first one I will tell you will be about Deborah. Before the Israelites had any kings, they used to have chiefs and judges to rule over them. And in the time of the judges, there was all kinds of trouble.

The Israelites never looked for a fight or for war—they did not want it—they wanted to live a quiet, peaceful life. But there were many people living in the country all around them, who were wild and rough and who always wanted to fight or have war. And these rough neighbors worried the Israelites very much and very often; so the judges had to be very wise in order to settle all the troubles.

One of the very best of the judges was a woman, and her name was Deborah. She lived in a tent which

DEBORAH

THE WOMAN JUDGE

was set under a large palm tree near Mount Ephraim. Do you remember how Abraham used to sit at the door of his tent? And do you remember how all the people came to him, and how he always settled their quarrels? Well, Deborah did the same thing, and the people came to her with all their troubles.

Deborah lived in a warm country, where there was no winter, no snow or ice, and no cold weather at all. And there Deborah sat by the door of her tent, in the shade of that large and beautiful palm tree. The tree was known as "Deborah's Palm," and all the people, even if they lived many , many miles away, knew that they could always find Deborah sitting there. They knew that Deborah was good and wise, and they knew whatever she told them to do, would be the right thing.

Deborah could settle the little quarrels, but often, the wild tribes who lived in the mountains, hundreds and thousands of them, would come to fight the Israelites. Deborah knew she must have an army, too, who could fight these wild neighbors. So she ordered all the men to come to a great meeting, and when they were all together, she formed them into an army, just as easily as the boys in the street form a little company of make-believe soldiers, only Deborah's men were really soldiers.

One day she sent for Barak, the general of the army. When he came she said to him: "Our neighbors are giving us too much trouble. Call the officers and all the soldiers together, and go out to fight."

"If you will go with the army," said Barak, "I will go too; but I will not go without you." Just think of that—a brave, strong general, to say to a woman that he would not go to war without her! But can you guess why he said it? Not because Barak was afraid, but because he knew how wise and good Deborah was, and he wanted her there to help the soldiers and cheer them up.

Deborah said: "I will go with you, but you will not need me. The God of Israel is always on the side of the Right, and we are in the right. Sisera, the general of the other army is a very wicked man, and we will win in this fight."

And what Deborah said came true. She stood on a little hill near the field of battle, and she saw that the Israelites were winning. When the battle was over, Deborah commanded the bugler to sound the bugle call that brought the soldiers together. He did this,

THE WOMAN JUDGE

and when they formed in companies all around Deborah, and wanted to cheer for her, she held up her hand for silence. Then she sang a song of praise and thanks to God, for letting the Israelites win the battle, and in it she prayed God always to be good to His children.

Some day, when you are older, you can read the words of this song in the Bible.

XII

A STORY OF LOVE

RUTH

Do you remember about the famine, long ago, when Joseph was the governor of Egypt, the time when there was very little to eat in the whole country? Well, in the time of the Judges, long after Deborah died, there was a great famine, too. In one town, many people packed their things and moved away. In this town there lived a man named Elimelech, with his wife Naomi, and their two sons.

When Elimelech saw how little food there was, he told his family they must move away from the place. They went to the country of Moab where there was plenty of everything, and made their home there. When the two sons were old enough, they married two young girls, Orpah and Ruth, who lived in Moab. After awhile Elimelech died, and Naomi went to live with her children who had their own house.

But poor Naomi was sad all the time, for she missed

A STORY OF LOVE

her good husband and her own land. She could not speak to any one in Moab, because she did not understand the language. Orpah and Ruth had tried to learn a little Hebrew, so as to talk with Naomi, but they did not know very much. Naomi was very homesick too, and often wished she could go back to her old home.

One day Naomi's son was taken very sick and died. Soon after that, the other son was taken sick in the same way, and he died too. Can you imagine how unhappy Naomi was? Her husband and her two dear sons were all dead, and she was alone in a strange city, far, far away from her home and her relations. Of course, she had Orpah and Ruth, but they were not her very own. They belonged in Moab, and Naomi thought that now both girls would go back to their fathers' houses.

One day Naomi and the two girls were sitting together in their room. Naomi said: "It is many years since I came to Moab to stay here, and now there is no more famine in my own land. I am an old woman, and I want to go back to my home and my people. I want to be where I can pray to God in my own old way, and that is very different from your way here in Moab."

The girls said they would go with her, but Naomi

answered: "No, no. I am old and you are young. You stay here in your own country, with all your friends, with people you know and love." Naomi took her handkerchief and dried her eyes. Then she spoke again: "You have been good girls. You have been good wives to your husbands, my dear sons, and you have been kind to me. I ask my God to bless you both. My clothes are all packed and I am going now, so I will say goodbye to both of you."

Orpah kissed Naomi many times and left her. But Ruth stood still and said: "I cannot leave you alone, dear mother Naomi."

"See, Ruth," said Naomi, "Orpah has gone back to her people; won't you go, too?"

But Ruth threw her young strong arms around the neck of the lovely old Naomi, kissed her, and begged her to let her go back to Bethlehem to the old home with her.

Naomi shook her head and said, "No, no," once more, but Ruth answered: "Entreat me not to leave thee, or to return from following after thee. Whither thou goest, I will go and where thou lodgest I will lodge. Thy people shall be my people and thy God my God."

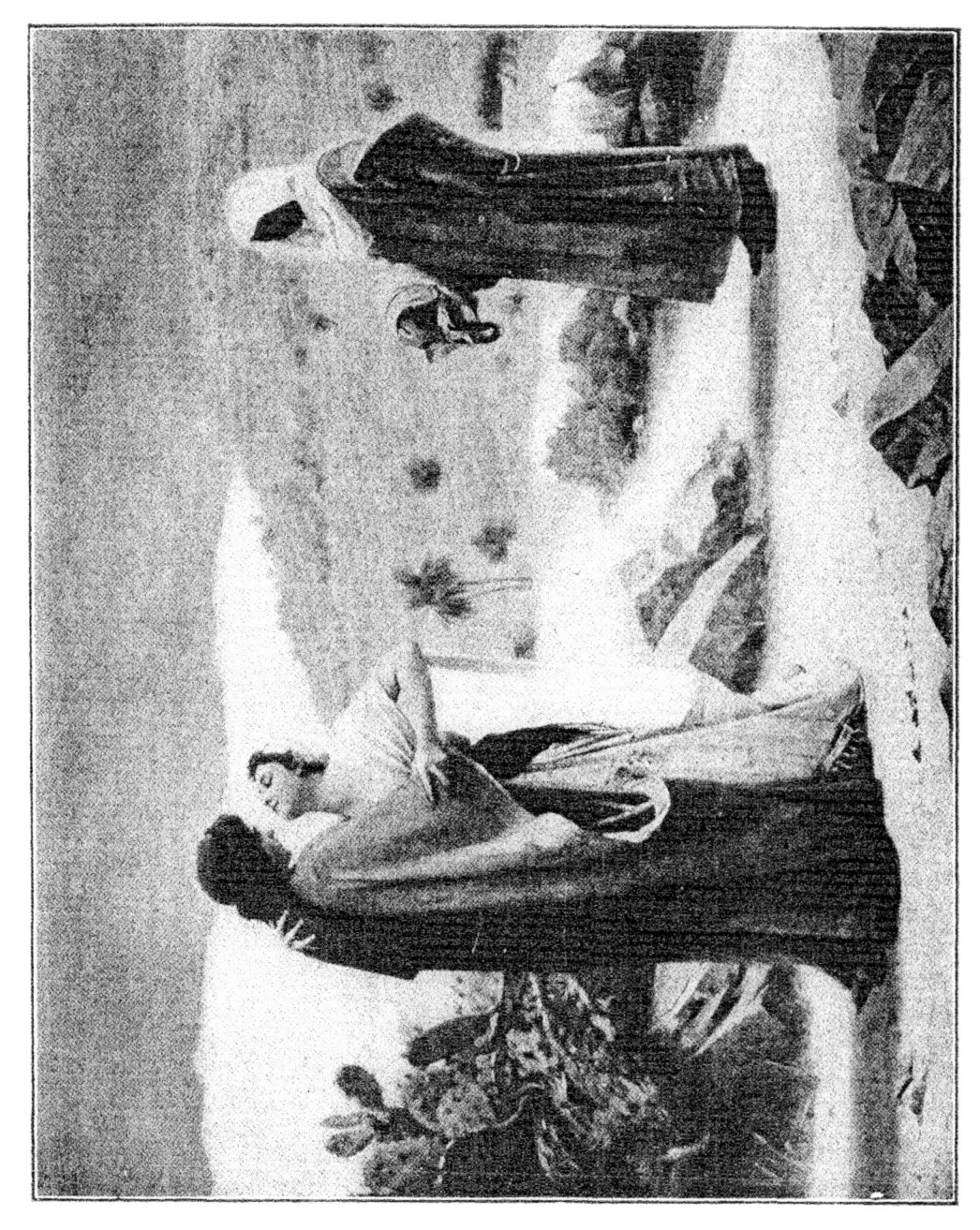

RUTH, THROWING HER ARMS AROUND NAOMI, SAID: "ENTREAT ME NOT TO LEAVE THEE."

A STORY OF LOVE

Those are the beautiful words and sentences, just as they are printed in the Bible. I put them in the story because I want you to know them. But perhaps some of the little folks who hear or read these stories will not understand what Ruth meant, so I will tell you again in another way. Ruth said to Naomi:

"Please do not send me away from you. Let me follow you, and let me go to your home to live there with you. I want your people to love me, just as if they were my own people. I want you to teach me to pray to your God, so He can be my God too."

Wasn't that just lovely of Ruth to talk like that to Naomi? But Ruth loved Naomi as much as any of you love your own dear Mama. That was why she would not let her go away all alone.

When Naomi saw that Ruth was in earnest, and loved her enough to go away with her, she was very glad. She never said to either of the girls, how scared she was to take that long journey to Bethlehem from Moab all alone, and she was happy to have Ruth for company.

They came to Bethlehem just at the time when the grain was ripe. All the fields were filled with men and women. The rich men who owned all the corn and barley and wheat had sent out their servants and all the men who worked on the farms, to cut down the grain. When it was all cut down and dried by the sun, it was brought home and put away in the barns.

Naomi had a cousin who lived in Bethlehem—a very rich man whose name was Boaz. Boaz owned many fields and he had many men and women working there for him, to cut down the grain and to put it away in the barns.

Now there was a law that Moses had given to his people long ago at the time that he made all the laws for them, and it was this: When the ripe grain is cut down in the fields, no one dare touch any grain that grows in the corners—the four corners of the field, this grain must be left for the poor.

Was not that a kind law? Men who were poor, did not own land and had no grain, so when the servants of the rich men left the grain in the four corners of the fields, the poor people had the right to go there at certain times and pick it all up. This law was obeyed by every one who owned fields of grain, and the servants of Boaz were told to leave the grain alone that grew in the corners.

A STORY OF LOVE

For a few days after Ruth and Noami had come to Bethlehem, Ruth watched the men and women at work in the fields. Then she said to Naomi: "May I go out into the fields to pick some barley?"

Naomi said: "Yes, you may go for we are very poor, and there is much grain left in the corners. And Ruth, I want you to go to the fields that belong to my cousin Boaz, and gather the barley there."

Boaz had never seen Ruth before, so when he saw her in the field, standing in the corner and placing the barley in her apron, he asked one of his servants: "Who is that strange girl? I have never seen her before."

"That is Ruth—the beautiful young woman from Moab. She left her home and all her people to come here with Naomi, and to take care of her because she is old and lonely."

Boaz said to his servants: "Leave plenty of barley in the corners, and whoever goes near Ruth must drop some of the barley on the ground near her , so that she can see it and pick it up."

One day, when Boaz was walking across the field, he spoke to Ruth, and said: "Tell me why do you stand in the sun all day? You work as hard as my servants do."

"Because I love Naomi," answered Ruth. "She is poor, and she is too old to work. So I am gathering all the grain I can."

Boaz looked at the pretty girl for a moment, and then said: "At noontime, go and sit by the other girls and eat the food that they brought with them."

He went to his servants and told them to give her something to eat at noon, and to be very kind to her. Then he went back to the house, for Boaz was a very rich man, and had a fine house. He thought of Ruth many times that day, and said to himself: "Ruth is a beautiful girl, and she is as good and as kind and as helpful as she is beautiful."

Boaz was lonely in his big house, all alone with his servants. One day he went to see his cousin Naomi and asked her to come and live in his house. He said: "I love your daughter Ruth and I want to marry her, and then you both can live with me."

Ruth loved Boaz too, so they were married; and the poor girl from Moab became the rich lady of Bethlehem. But she always remained the same kind-hearted, sweet and helpful Ruth, and was good to the poor, and did whatever she could for them.

XIII

THE BOY PRIEST

SAMUEL

Many years after the death of Joshua, in a small town near Shiloh, there lived a man named Elkanah and his wife Hannah. They loved God very much, and prayed to Him every morning and every night, and Hannah talked to God just like you talk to your father.

Once she prayed to God to send her a little baby boy, and said: "Dear God, if you send me a little baby boy, you will make me very happy. Just as soon as he is old enough to walk, I will let him go to Shiloh, and be a priest like Aaron was."

Shiloh was the city where the Israelites used to go to bring sacrifices. They worshipped God in the Tabernacle; and Eli was the name of the head priest there, or "high priest," as he was called. The Tabernacle was something like a temple, only not so fine, and the priests lived near there.

One day the little baby boy that Hannah had prayed for, came to her home. She named him Samuel. She was very happy to have this little baby for he was good and sweet and pretty. Although Hannah loved her little boy very much, she did not forget her promise, and when Samuel was two years old, his father and mother took him to Shiloh to the Tabernacle.

The good old priest Eli was sitting near the gate, and said to Hannah: "Who is that little child? Why do you bring him here?" Hannah answered: "I prayed to God once to send me this little boy, and I promised he should learn to serve God and be a priest. I have brought him here to keep my promise, and will leave him here to serve in the Tabernacle."

Eli told little Samuel to kiss his mother good-bye, after which she went back to her home. Eli took the little boy with him to his own house. He showed Samuel a small room with a tiny bed, and a chair and table in it, and said: "This will be your own little room. I sleep in the next room. If you want me at night you can call me, and I will come to you. If I want you for anything, I will call you to come to me."

Samuel was happy in the house of the good priest Eli,

HANNAH BRINGS HER LITTLE BOY SAMUEL TO ELI

THE BOY PRIEST

and he was such a cheerful, good and merry little fellow that every one loved him. But though he liked to play, just like other little boys do, he loved to go to the Tabernacle with Eli, and always helped the kind old priest in every way he could.

Once every year, Samuel's father and mother came to Shiloh to worship God, and every year Hannah brought a nice new coat for her boy. And as the boy grew older, he was tall and beautiful. He was kind to every one and was now very helpful to Eli. He helped him more with the sacrifices and the prayers every day.

One night, while Samuel was asleep, he thought he heard some one call his name. He jumped out of bed, went into Eli's room and said: "Here I am,—I heard you call me,"

"But I did not call you," said Eli. "Go back to bed again."

Samuel obeyed, but soon afterward, the boy heard his name called again. He jumped up, hurried into Eli's room, and asked what Eli wanted.

Eli said he did not call, and sent the boy back to bed. In a little while, he heard the call again. Again he hurried into Eli's room and told him. Then Eli knew it was God who was calling the boy, and he said to Samuel: "Go back to bed once more, and when you hear the voice again, you must answer, because it is God who called you."

Samuel did as Eli said, and it did not take long before he heard the call again: "Samuel! Samuel!"

"I am here, O God," said the boy.

Then God told Samuel that Eli was a very old man and would die soon, and that God wanted Samuel to be the priest afterwards. So, after Eli's death Samuel was the high priest, and he taught the people many good and wise things.

After the Israelites came into the Promised Land, they chose different places where they put up their tents for their homes. They planted many kinds of fruit trees and nut trees, and all kinds of grain, mostly wheat and barley and oats. They tended their sheep and goats and cattle, and lived a quiet peaceful life for many years.

But they had some neighbors living in different towns near there, who often made trouble for them. The Israelites had good laws, and they had chiefs to rule. These chiefs were called Priests and Judges. But the

THE BOY PRIEST

Israelites thought if they had a king, the neighbors would be afraid of him, and then they would not be so troublesome.

So the Judges called a meeting of the men of all the tribes of Israel to talk it over. They had the meeting and chose a man named Saul to be their king. Samuel was sorry for this. He knew there was many a man in Israel who would be a better king than Saul, but he did not say what he thought.

After Saul was king for awhile, he said and did many things that were not right. Then God called to Samuel, and said to him: "You know Saul is not a very good man, so you must have another king. There is a family of very good men in Bethlehem, and one of that family is to be King of Israel. Go to Jesse, who is the head of the family, and ask him to let you talk to all his sons. Then I will tell you which one shall be king."

Samuel went to Jesse's home, and asked to see the sons. Jesse called them one after the other, until seven fine men stood before Samuel. Then Samuel asked: "Is this all? Have you no other son?"

"There is only one more," answered Jesse, "but he is a young boy and takes care of the sheep."

"Send for him, so that I can see him," said Samuel.

When the boy came, Samuel saw how beautiful he was. He also heard the Voice of God saying: "This is the boy David, whom I want for the King of Israel. Go now, get some holy oil, pour a little on his head and anoint him with it."

Then Samuel took a horn filled with the holy oil. He poured a few drops on the boy's head, rubbed it into his hair, and said a little prayer. In former times this was always done when a new king was chosen.

Now, Saul was very sorry for the wrong things he had done, and he promised he would obey all God's commandments and be a good king. So, although David had been made the real king, when the holy oil was put on his head, just now Saul was king.

XIV

THE SHEPHERD KING

DAVID

The nearest neighbors to the Israelites were the Philistines. These people wanted the rich land that belonged to the Israelites, so the king of the Philistines went to war against the king of the Israelites. The Philistines were all very large and tall men, many of them were giants. The king of the Philistines had placed his army on the side of a tall mountain. Saul's army was on the side of another mountain. Between these two mountains there were smooth fields, called a valley.

One morning, a man from the Philistine army came down the mountain-side, and went out into the valley. The man was a big giant, and his name was Goliath. He had a heavy brass helmet on his head, his coat was made of little pieces of steel joined together, and he had metal coverings on his arms and legs. In one hand he carried a big shield, in the other hand he held a spear that was as high as a lamp-post, and hanging down from a wide leather belt, was a very long sword.

Goliath looked so fierce and ugly, it was enough to frighten anybody. He looked around him at the two armies on the two mountains, and then shouted in a voice as loud as thunder: "I am a Philistine. You are the soldiers of Saul, king of Israel. Send a man down here in the valley to fight with me. If he wins the fight and kills me, all the Philistines will be your servants and work for you. But, if I win and kill your man, all the Israelites must be our servants and work for us. Now, send down your man!"

Saul and his soldiers heard what Goliath said, but they were afraid to send any man down, because they had no tall men in their army who could fight such a great big giant. And every morning, Goliath stalked out into the valley to shout the same words, but no man was willing to fight with him.

The brothers of David were in Saul's army, and every day young David came into the camp of Israel to bring food to his brothers. When he heard what Goliath was shouting, David said: "I am not afraid.

THE SHEPHERD KING

I will fight with him." Saul told him he was too young, and was not strong enough, but David said: "I know I am young, but I am strong. Once a lion came into the field where I was watching my father's sheep. The lion took a lamb, and I killed the lion. Another time a bear came and tried to take one of the sheep, and I killed him too."

"If you were able to kill the lion and the bear," said the king, "I am sure you are not afraid of this giant. Go, and may God take care of you."

Saul gave David his own heavy coat of steel and iron, and his own helmet and sword. Can you imagine how funny little David looked after he dressed himself in a man's clothes? He felt as funny as he looked. He thanked the king, then took off the things and said they were too big and too heavy for him to wear. Then he picked up his staff, that is, the little stick with which he used to keep the sheep together, and walked away.

David went over to a little stream that flowed down the mountain-side. There he found five smooth stones, and he put them in a little bag he carried. In his hand he held a sling,—a kind of heavy cord with a loose knot at the end. If a stone is put carefully into a good sling, it can be thrown at any one with very much force.

David ran down into the valley, and when the giant saw the little fellow he laughed out loud, and said: "Is this the man you people of Israel send out to fight with me? He is nothing but a boy, and I will show you how easily I can kill him."

David said: "You come to me with a sword and a spear, but I come to you in the name of the Lord our God of Israel. He will give me strength to kill you even if I am a little boy, for God is on our side."

David quickly took a stone from his bag, fastened it in the sling, and threw it with all his might. The stone struck the giant right in the middle of his forehead, and it hurt him so much that he fell down upon the ground. What a noise it made when that big man, with his heavy spear and sword and shield, and his steel coat and brass helmet all fell on the ground together!

David ran over to where Goliath fell, stooped down, and pulled the giant's own sword out of its case. It was very heavy but David pulled hard. And with that big sword he cut off the giants' head.

The Philistine soldiers were so much suprised to see that little boy go out to fight Goliath, that they all stood

THE SHEPHERD KING

still to watch him. But when they saw that their great man was dead, they all ran away. The soldiers of Israel shouted for joy, and chased them far out of the country; and that was the end of the war.

David went back to the camp, and Saul said to him: "Who are you? and what is your father's name?"

"I am David," said the boy. "My father's name is Jesse, and we live in Bethlehem."

Saul liked David, and he sent word to Jesse that he wanted David to stay with him. David had a very sweet voice, and could sing many songs, and they sometimes called him the sweet singer of Israel. He could play on the harp very well, and whenever Saul was tired or worried, he asked David to play and sing for him.

Now King Saul had a son whose name was Prince Jonathan, and Jonathan and David soon were the best friends. In those old times when a king or a prince loved any one very much and wanted him for a friend, the king or the prince took off something of his own and gave it to the friend. Do you remember how that good king Pharaoh took off his gold chain from his own neck and gave it to Joseph? So, Prince Jonathan took off his fine cloak, and gave it to David, and also gave him his sword and belt, and his bow and arrows. And they promised each other always to be friends.

David obeyed Saul and behaved so well that Saul made him a captain in the army. It did not take long before the soldiers loved Captain David more than they did King Saul. This made Saul angry, and one day when David was playing on the harp and singing, Saul threw his spear at David and nearly hit him. If that heavy spear had hit David, it might have killed him. David left the room and went to look for Jonathan.

After David told Jonathan all about it, he asked: "What have I done that King Saul wants to hurt me? He might have killed me with that spear."

"I am sure," said Jonathan, "that my father does not want to kill you. Is there anything I can do for you?"

"I will not go back to the palace now," David said, "but I want to stay with you for a few days. I want you to talk to your father about me, and then tell me what he says. I think King Saul does not like me any more."

"I have often told you, David," said Jonathan,

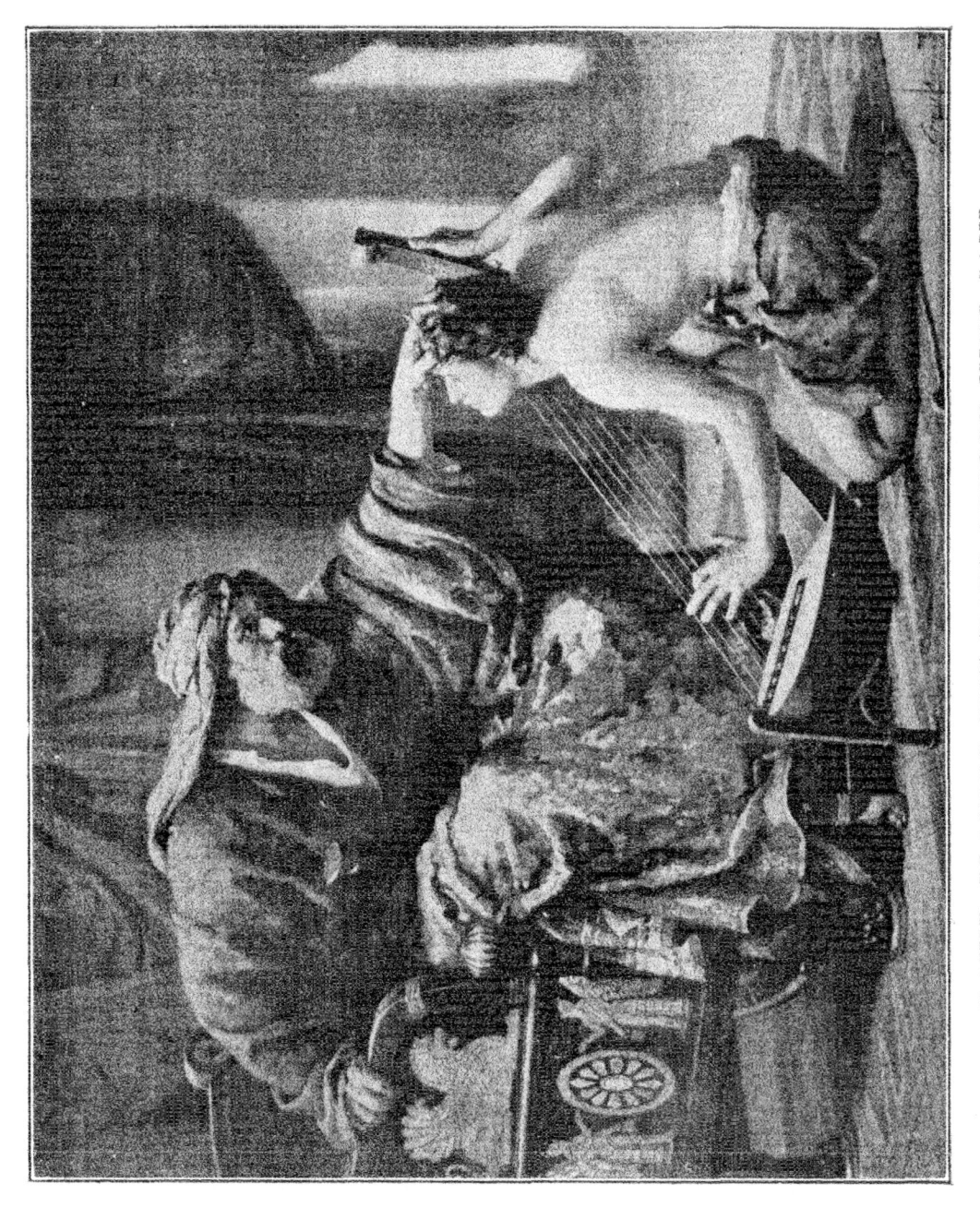

DAVID PLAYING THE HARP BEFORE KING SAUL

"that I love you and will always be your friend. True friends always try to help each other, and I will help you all I can."

Jonathan went to his father, and told him David was going away. He begged his father to tell David to come back, and said: "I love David and he is good and kind. I beg you to send for him to stay here."

But Saul would not, and Jonathan was very unhappy when he left his father's room. He did not like to tell David that Saul did not like him any more, but he had to do so. And when David went away, Jonathan and David kissed each other many times, and both of them were very sad to think they would not see each other again.

The neighboring tribes always gave Saul much trouble, and after David went away, another war began. And in one of the battles, both Saul and Jonathan were killed.

When the news was told to David, he was very sorry, for he knew that now he would never see his dear friend Jonathan any more. David wrote some very nice verses about his friend. They are in the Bible, in the part called "The Second Book of Samuel."

David was now the real king of Israel. He soon stopped all the wars. He began to build a city, the city of Jerusalem, and he sent for all the people of Israel to come there to live. He taught them how to pray, and he was the first man who thought of building a Temple. David had wished to build a great temple in Jerusalem, but he did not live long enough. His son Solomon built it afterwards.

When David was quite an old man, he said he was tired of being king. He wanted his son Solomon to be king instead of him. But David had another son named Absalom. Absalom wanted to be the king, so he called all his friends together and said: "My father is too old to be king any longer. Would you like to have me for your king?"

Absalom was a very handsome young man, with big blue eyes and golden curls that came down to his shoulders. All the men who came to the meeting were his friends.

"Yes," said the men, "we want you for our king, because King David is too old."

Absalom said: "Then go all through the land, and say to every one you meet 'Absalom is king.'"

THE SHEPHERD KING

When David heard about this, he was very angry, for David had said Solomon was to be king, and now Absalom had disobeyed him. So David called his soldiers out, told them to look for Absalom and his friends, and bring them back as prisoners. It was a very large company of soldiers that David sent to look for Absalom and his friends, and they found Absalom in a thick forest.

When Absalom saw his father's soldiers coming into the woods where he was hiding, Absalom was frightened. When he saw how all his friends were caught and made prisoners he was badly scared. He knew how wicked he had been, and he was afraid to be taken prisoner, and brought back to the king. He saw a mule tied to a tree near him. He untied the rope and jumped on his back. He thought he could ride away so fast, that the soldiers could not catch him.

And then a dreadful thing happened. You know Absalom had long, curly hair, and when he was riding so fast his hair flew back in the wind. As he was riding along his hair caught in the branch of a tree. It pulled him off the mule so roughly that it broke his neck!

Wasn't that horrible? And yet Absalom deserved

the punishment because he did very wrong. First, he disobeyed his father's wishes, for he knew that his father wished Solomon to be king. Then he called all his friends to help him fight against his father. When the soldiers came back and told King David, he cried and sobbed to think that his son Absalom whom he loved so much, was dead.

XV

THE WISE KING

SOLOMON

From the time that Solomon was a small boy, his father, King David, made him study, and Solomon loved to learn. He learned to read and write and spell just like any other little boy. When he was older he studied all about the sun and moon and stars, and about rocks and trees and flowers, and about animals and birds and insects.

One night Solomon had a strange dream. He dreamed that he heard the Voice of God saying: "Ask for something that I shall give you."

And Solomon answered: "You were good to my father David, and you have been good to me. I am king now, but sometimes I feel like a little child who cannot understand things. I want to be a good king to my people, so I beg this of you. Make me wise. Give me wisdom to rule the people well, and to judge for them. And teach me to know the difference between right and wrong. This is all I ask."

Solomon might have wished for all kinds of nice things, but you see, all he asked for was wisdom. That pleased God, who said: "Because you wished for wisdom, when you might have wished for money or long life or many other things, I will give you your wish. I will give you a wise heart and head to understand all things. I will also give you the things you did not ask for—I will give you riches and honor and greatness."

This was Solomon's dream, but it all came true. God made Solomon so wise that he understood what the little birds said when they chirped or sang in their pretty nests in the trees, and he understood what the animals said when they roared or growled or cried out. He also knew what the trees were saying when the little leaves shook and when the big branches swung up and down in the wind.

Solomon was a very wise judge. A judge is a man who settles any quarrel. When some men had a quarrel, about cattle or houses or lands they owned, if they could not agree, they went to Solomon and told him.

"OH, GREAT KING, DO NOT CUT MY CHILD IN TWO,"
CRIED THE REAL MOTHER TO SOLOMON

THE WISE KING

Solomon listened to them quietly, settled the business for them, and the men went home perfectly satisfied.

Once two women quarreled. Each woman had a little baby, but afterwards, one baby was taken sick and died. The woman whose baby died, wanted a little baby so much, that she took the baby that belonged to the other woman, and she kept it. She would not give it back to its own mother. After they had quarreled a long time about it, the real mother said they should take the baby to King Solomon, and let him settle it.

When they stood before the king, each woman said "this is my baby." Solomon sent for a soldier, and when he came, Solomon said: "Take your sword. Cut the baby in two pieces, and give a piece to each woman."

One woman cried out: "Oh, great king, do not cut my little child in two. Give it to that woman. I would rather give her my own dear baby, than let your soldier hurt it."

The other woman said. "Great king, you may cut the child in two pieces if you want to. I don't care."

Which woman do you think was the real mother?

Yes, the woman who would not let them hurt the baby. And Solomon gave her the little child, and punished the other woman.

Now I will tell you about the wonderful temple that King Solomon gave orders to build, which is still called "The Temple of Solomon."

Solomon loved God very much, and he wanted this temple to be the most beautiful thing that ever was made. So he sent men all through the forests for wood. He told them to cut down the largest and finest trees they could find—cedar trees, fir trees, and olive trees—and bring them back to the city. He sent other men to the mountains, to dig out great rocks of granite and marble and onyx, and bring them into the city. And other men were sent to the mines, to get gold and silver and copper and precious stones.

Then they began to build this great House of God. They took the largest rocks, cut them into big, smooth blocks, and used them for the cellar and the outside walls. They used the fine wood for the roof and doors and window-frames. The windows were made of colored glass, and they had every pretty color you can think of. The pillars, that is, the posts that held

THE WISE KING

the roof up—were made out of pure white marble and onyx. All the decorations or trimmings in the whole building, were made out of real gold and silver.

The altar was made of cedar-wood and then covered with gold. The ark that held the Holy Law was made of gold and precious stones. The altar was separated from the rest of the temple by heavy chains of solid gold. On the ceiling, and on all the doors, were fine pictures cut into the wood. This is called carving, and the carvings in the temple were of angels and flowers, and everything was ornamented with gold. It took seven years to build the temple.

When the temple was finished, King Solomon sent for all the chiefs and captains and all the people of Israel, to come to Jerusalem to dedicate the temple. (To dedicate a temple means to ask God to bless the temple, and to bless all the people who come there to pray and to worship God.)

When all the people came, Solomon prayed an earnest prayer to God. He asked God to take care of the temple, and to watch over all the people, and to make the leaders good and brave.

When Solomon had finished this prayer, he blessed

the whole congregation and said: "May the Lord, our God, be with us, as He always was with our fathers. May we always love Him, and may He ever help us to keep His commandments. And may all the people in the whole world know, that the Lord is God, and there is no other God."

Every one left the temple after Solomon ended the blessing. But they did not go to their homes because the king had invited them to a great feast. All the people stayed in Jerusalem the rest of that day, and all were happy and contented.

King Solomon was the richest man in the world. Besides the wonderful temple that he built, he built a fine palace for himself out of pure white marble, and he built a magnificent court-house. He also built a high stone wall around the city of Jerusalem. He owned many cities and many ships that sailed on the sea.

Everybody in that part of the world had heard about Solomon, and the wise things that he did. Many people came to visit him just to see if what they had heard was true. And these people brought with them many presents made of silver and gold and jewels for the king. Three times a year King Solomon himself offered sacrifices

THE WISE KING

in the court-yard of the temple, and thousands of people came there to worship God.

In a country very far away from Jerusalem, there lived a queen, beautiful and rich and wise and good. She was the Queen of Sheba, and many people had heard of her and traveled in her country. They told of all the wonderful things that Solomon had done, what a good, wise king he was, and how he loved and worshiped God. The Queen of Sheba wanted to find out if all these things were true, so she made up her mind to go and visit King Solomon.

She told her officers to get gold and jewels for presents to take with her. The servants brought a long train of camels, they were loaded with all that was needed for the journey, and they started for Jerusalem. It was a very long way, and they had to ride many miles through a hot, dry, sandy desert, where there were no trees, nor grass, nor water, nothing but the hot sun and the sandy ground.

At last, they reached Jerusalem. They saw the great wall, the wonderful temple, and all the other fine buildings. And at a distance, Solomon's marble palace shone in the sunshine like diamonds. Solomon came to the gates of the city to meet the queen, and he showed her everything she wanted to see. He invited her to come to his palace and stay there as long as she liked.

She went to the palace, and saw the king's throne that was made out of ivory and gold, and the golden chairs. She looked through the finely-painted windows, each one different from the other, and all of them were painted in many colors. When they sat down to dinner in the marble dining-hall, the queen saw that all the dishes and spoons and knives and forks were made of pure gold.

After the meal was over, Solomon took the queen into the temple, and she saw that everything was true that she had heard. When they were going out of the temple into the court-yard, the queen noticed a brass trumpet that was as long as the side of a small house. She stood still before it, and said: "I did not hear about this. Is it a trumpet? What is the good of it?"

"No one knows how good it is, and no one knows how much good it does." said Solomon.

"Why, what do you mean?" said the queen. "How can a trumpet do any good?"

Solomon answered: "You have seen many beauti-

THE WISE KING

ful things that have cost much money, and you have met very many rich people here in Jerusalem. But there are very many poor people here, too. Long ago, when Moses made laws for the children of Israel, he said the rich people must help the poor. Moses said: 'We must give all that we can to the poor; not because we think we are doing a good deed, but because it is right for us to help them.' That is why I had this trumpet made and placed here."

Solomon then told the queen how the trumpet had been made, and said: "The rich person stands in front of the great mouth of the trumpet, and puts in some money or food or clothing or anything he wants to give away. The different things slide down the trumpet to the small end, where the poor people stand. Each one gets his turn, and takes out the things that the rich men put into the large end. The trumpet was made so wide at the large end that the rich people cannot see the poor ones, and the poor ones never know who gave them help."

"Indeed you are a great and wise king," said the queen. "I did not believe half of what they told me about you, but now I know how good you are. There were many good and wise things you do that no one told me, because they did not know. Ah! Solomon, how happy your people must be with such a king to rule over them."

When, in a few days, the Queen of Sheba said she must go home, Solomon gave her so many presents that her camels had very heavy loads to carry. After the queen said good-bye to King Solomon, she held his hand and said: "I have been thinking about it, and I know now why you are so rich. It is because you are wise, and know how to rule the people. It is because you love your God and pray to Him. That is the reason why He has always helped you, and blessed you."

XVI

THE MAN OF GOD

DANIEL

You have surely all seen that old picture of a man in a cage full of lions, where the lions did not hurt the man at all. The name of the picture is: "Daniel in the Lions' Den." Did you not know the story about it is in the Bible? Well, it is, and there are other things about that same Daniel, which you shall hear now.

There was a country called Babylon, and the king of that country was named Nebuchadnezzar. (Isn't that a pretty hard name?) There had been a war, and Nebuchadnezzar took many men as his prisoners. Daniel was one of the prisoners. Daniel had three friends who were also taken prisoners. The king soon found out that Daniel and his friends were all wise men who had studied and learned very much, so he gave orders to the captain of his guards to be kind to them.

But though these men were prisoners, the king often

sent for them when he was bothered about something, so that they might tell him what to do. You remember how Joseph used to explain dreams, and Daniel could do the same thing. One night the king had a dream. In the morning when he awoke, he had forgotten what the dream was. He tried to think about it but he could not remember anything, except that it was a dream he did not understand, and it worried him.

All the kings used to have wise men to explain their dreams, so Nebuchadnezzar sent for his wise men. When they were all in the palace the king said: "I had a dream last night, so I sent for you to explain it."

"What was your dream, great king?" asked the wise men. "Tell us so that we can explain it."

"Oh," answered the king, "I have forgotten what the dream was."

"But, great king, how can we explain the dream if you cannot tell us what is was? Please try to think."

"I cannot think," said the king. "You say you are wise men, and if you cannot tell me what my dream was I will not have you any more. So you may go and I will give an order to my officers to drive all the wise men out of my country."

THE MAN OF GOD

The king gave this foolish order, and the officers went to Daniel and his friends, because they were wise men, too. They told Daniel the king had commanded that all the wise men must be sent out of the land. Daniel said to the officers: "Do not do this now. Do not send us away yet. Let me speak to the king first. Ask him if I may go to him tomorrow morning."

After the officers had gone away, Daniel said to his friends: "If God does not help us now, the king will drive us away out into the desert. So let us all pray tonight to God. Let us ask Him to watch over us and take care of us. Let us thank God for all His goodness to us, and for the wisdom He gave us."

Daniel's friends went to their own rooms, and when Daniel was alone he prayed to God again, and said: "Oh God, I pray you, give me the same dream tonight that Nebuchadnezzar had last night, and then I can explain it to the king."

And God loved Daniel and answered his prayer, and that night Daniel dreamed the same dream that the king had dreamed the night before. When Daniel awoke the next morning his first thought was of God, and he said: "I thank you and praise you, God of my fathers, for your goodness to me, and because you sent me this dream. Now I can tell it to the king and nothing will happen to the wise men of Babylon, nor to my friends."

The officer that Daniel had sent to the king, now came again and told Daniel to go to the palace, for the king wanted him. Soon Daniel stood before the king who said: "Can you tell me what my dream was, and can you explain it?"

"No, king," said Daniel. "I cannot, but my God can."

"What do you mean?" asked the king, and Daniel said: "There are many things that no one can explain—neither the wise men, nor the teachers, nor the priests. But there is a God in heaven, who has helped me understand your dream and now I can explain it to you."

For a moment Daniel was still. Then he said: "You dreamed you saw a statue or image of a great, tall man. The head was made of gold, the breast and arms were silver, the body was brass, the legs were iron, and the feet were clay. Suddenly a heavy stone fell through the air, and hit the statue on the feet. The feet were made of clay and when the stone struck them they broke to pieces, just like a cup would break. Then the great big statue

DANIEL IN THE DEN OF WILD LIONS

THE MAN OF GOD

fell down, and was broken and bent and spoiled. And in the dream you saw how the stone was changed into a high mountain."

"Yes," answered King Nebuchadnezzar, "that was my dream; and now tell me quickly what it all means, for I do not know."

"O king," said Daniel, "the meaning is plain. The golden head means you, for that was the best part of the whole statue. You are a good king and you know how to govern the people, and your country is fine. After you are dead, there will be many other kings, but none of them will be good. In the statue that you saw in your dream, the silver came next to the gold. Silver is not as good as gold, and the next king after you will not be as good as you. Next to the silver came the brass, and then the iron, and last of all the clay. The brass and iron and clay mean other kings, each one worse than the other, and at last, just like the stone broke the clay feet and ruined the statue, this whole land will be ruined."

"But," said the king, "what does the stone mean, and why did it grow to be a mountain?"

"The stone means the people of Israel. There are

not very many of them here now, but there will be more and more, and when they are strong enough they will fight the people who always trouble them. When that time comes, they will conquer all their enemies and be as strong as a mountain. Then they will teach the world about the One, true God."

"Your God is a great God," said the king slowly, "and He made you very wise. I will make you ruler of one of my countries, and I will make your three friends rulers too."

Time passed on, and Nebuchadnezzar was taken sick. He could not rule over his land any more, so they had another king. The new king's name was Darius, and he loved Daniel so much, that he made him the chief over all the princes and officers. Of course, the princes and high officers did not like this, and they wished they knew something bad about Daniel to tell the king.

Daniel was so good that they could not find anything bad to tell, and they were afraid to make up a story, because they knew the king would punish them for telling him something that was not true. These men all knew that Daniel prayed to God three times a day—at morning, at noon, and at night. They knew too, that

THE MAN OF GOD

Daniel loved God more than he loved the king or any one else in the world.

So they went to King Darius with a plan. They talked to the king about it so much that he made this silly law: for thirty days no one was allowed to pray to God. Whoever did pray during this time, was to be thrown into a cage or den of wild lions. Everyone obeyed this law except Daniel. You see, that was what those bad men wanted—to get Daniel into trouble. They were sure Daniel would not obey such a law, and they thought that was a good way to make Darius angry at Daniel.

Just as if there was no new law about praying, Daniel kept on like he did before, and prayed three times every day. When the officers heard about it they went to the palace and told the king. Darius was very sorry because he loved Daniel, but he was very angry too, to think that Daniel did not obey the law. So he said: "Take him tonight and throw him into the lions' den. We will see if his God will save him."

So Daniel was pushed into the cage of wild lions, and the gate of the cage was locked. The king could not sleep that night because he was so sorry about Daniel, and so sure the lions would eat him up.

In the morning, very early, the king went to see what had happened. And what do you think? There was Daniel, safe and sound, lying by the lions who were all fast asleep!

And the king said: "And your God took care of you after all."

"King Darius," answered Daniel, "God is greater than any king. In the night He sent an angel to watch over me. When the lions saw the angel they became tame and did not hurt me. Then they went to sleep."

The king was very glad and took Daniel back to the palace with him, and said he should always stay there. He also punished the bad officers who had told him to make such a stupid and wicked law. Then the king thought of something he could do to make Daniel happy. He knew how dearly Daniel loved God and he had seen for himself how God watched over Daniel.

King Darius called all the people together to a big meeting. He told them what a great God there is in heaven above us, and how good He is to all who love Him. And Daniel taught the people how to pray and love God.

XVII

THE STORY OF CHANUKKAH

JUDAS MACCABBEUS

It was many hundred years after King Solomon built the beautiful Temple in Jerusalem. All the Jews in the land went to the Temple on Saturdays and holy days, to pray to God, to thank Him for His goodness, and to ask Him to take care of them. While Solomon lived the people were happy, because he was a wise and good king. Things were different after he died, and there were other kings who were not so wise and good as Solomon.

Often there was trouble for the Jews from the people who lived in other countries. These other people sometimes had a wicked king who liked to fight, and there were many wars. Some kings were not kind to the Jews and they were unhappy.

One king was very cruel. His name was Antiochus (An-ti-o-chus). He lived in a country called Syria.

He did so many wicked things that he was called the madman. Antiochus did not pray to the One God, as we do; he prayed to idols. An idol is an image which is made of wood, or stone, or iron. Sometimes it is in the shape of a man, and sometimes it is like an animal, or like a bird. King Antiochus bowed and prayed to his stupid images, and his people all did the same. All the people except the Jews, who knew better. The Jews prayed to God.

The king ordered the Jews to pray to the idols, like the others did. When they said they would not bow to idols, the king sent an army of soldiers to fight them. The king had so many soldiers, that they drove almost all of the Jews out of Jerusalem. When the poor Jews were gone, the soldiers climbed up the hill to where the wonderful Temple stood. They went into the Temple, took all the beautiful gold and silver ornaments and everything else that was in the Temple, and carried all away. Nothing was left but the roof and the walls.

Then some of the soldiers went off to find pigs, and when they had a big drove of them, they brought them to the Temple and chased them in. Do you know why they did this? For this reason: They knew the Jews

THE STORY OF CHANNUKAH

hated pigs because they are so dirty. I am sure you can imagine how angry, and sorry, and unhappy the Jews were when they heard that their loved Temple was full of pigs! Then Antiochus did another dreadful thing. He ordered an idol set up in a public place, where all the people passed very often, and he said every one must bow to it. Wasn't that wicked?

A few miles away from Jerusalem, there was a small town called Modin. An old man named Mattathias (Mat-ta-thi-as) lived there. He had five splendid sons, big, and brave, and good. Mattathias and his sons were very sorry for what had happened in Jerusalem, and they prayed that God would give strength to the Jews to win the Temple back again.

One day Mattathias went to Jerusalem, and when he saw that ugly idol, he was very angry at the king who ordered it to be put there in the street. While he was standing near it, he saw a Jewish man walk past the idol and bow down before it. Then Mattathias was more angry than before. He struck the other man and said:

"How dare you bow to an idol? Do you not know that is a sin? You know God said in His commandments, 'Thou shalt have no other God but me', and yet you do this wicked thing. You ought to be ashamed of yourself."

Mattathias would not stay in Jerusalem any longer. When he returned to his home in Modin, he told his sons and his neighbors what had happened. They were all as angry as Mattathias, and they asked:

"What are you going to do? Tell us and we will help you."

"We must raise an army of Jews," said Mattathias. "That is what we must do first; and when we have enough men, we are going to fight the soldiers of King Antiochus. We will drive them out of Jerusalem, for God will help us."

"Who will go to get the soldiers for us?" said one of the neighbors.

"We will go," said the sons of Mattathias.

They did as they said. The five sons went in different directions, and stopped in every house where Jews were living. In each house, the men were ready to go to fight for their religion, and before long they had quite a big army.

One of the sons of Mattathias was named Judas.

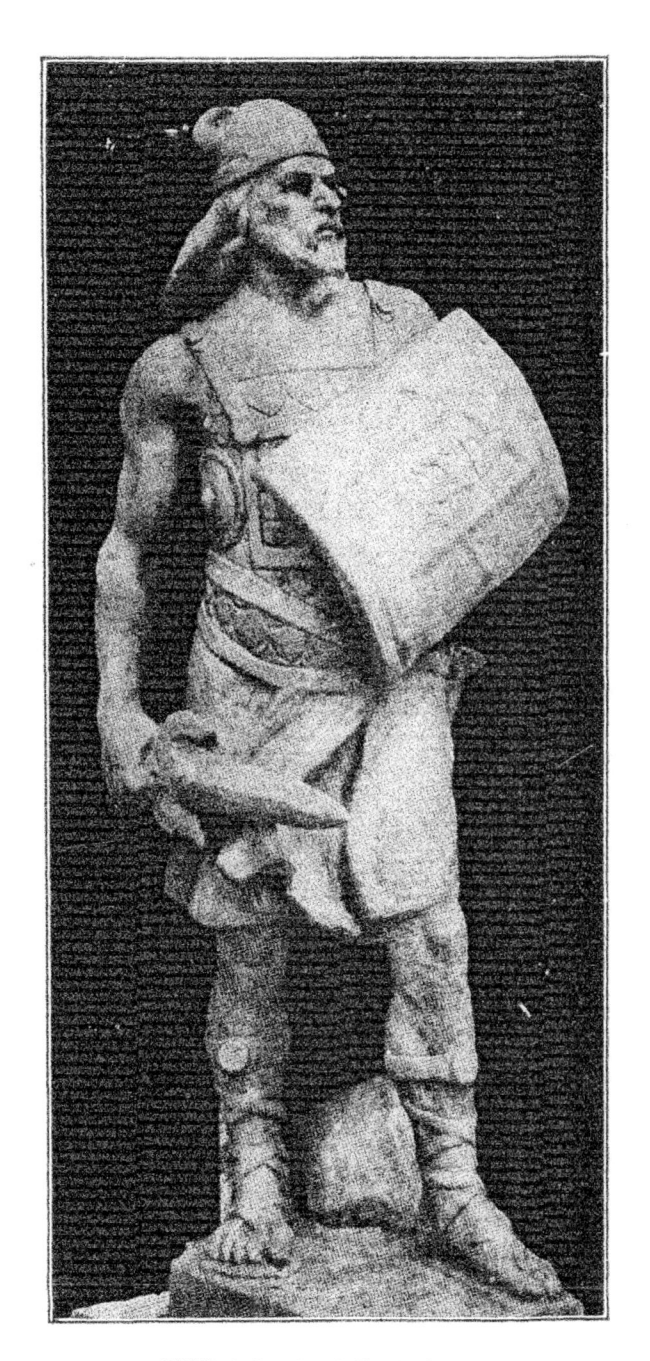

JUDAS MACCABBEUS
From the statue by Max Kalish

He was a big and handsome man, and people called him the Maccabbee, which means Hammer. He was so strong, that when he struck anything or anybody, it was like the blow of a hammer. Everybody loved him, and all the Jewish soldiers were pleased when Mattathias said Judas would be general of the army.

Judas Maccabbee had a banner made, which he carried into every fight. On the banner were the words "Mi Cho-mo-cho Bo-e-lim Ado-noi," which mean "Who is like Thee, O God, among the mighty?" The first letters of these words, in the Hebrew, spell MACCABBEE.

When his army saw that bright banner waving ahead of them, they followed it without any fear, for they knew Judas was there in the front ranks. On the road, they met many of the king's soldiers, and several small battles were fought before they reached Jerusalem. A big battle was fought in the city of Jerusalem. Judas Maccabbee conquered the king's soldiers and drove them out far past the city gates. Then they marched towards the Temple. When the Jewish soldiers saw how bad everything looked, they were very sad, but Judas said:

"This is no time to be sad. We should be glad, very glad. I am glad God gave us strength to drive away the enemy. I am glad the Temple is standing, even if it is empty and dirty. And I am glad we can clean it and make it beautiful again."

When his soldiers saw how cheerful Judas was, they smiled at him, and said:

"We are glad too, and we will all work hard to make this House of God look like it did before King Antiochus took it away from us."

You cannot imagine how busy they were and how hard the men worked. Some brought rakes to scrape the dirt from the walls and the floor. Some brought spades to shovel it up, and others brought big wooden boxes to carry all the rubbish away. When they had done all this, they called the women to come and help them; and they washed the windows, and cleaned the walls, and scrubbed the floors, till everything looked like new. When all was in good order, Judas said they must dedicate the Temple again, just as King Solomon had dedicated it hundreds of years before. (If you have forgotten what "dedicate" means, turn back to page 119.)

THE STORY OF CHANNUKAH

A lamp was hung over the altar in the Temple. Judas filled it with oil and lit it. Then he sent some soldiers around the country to all the Jews, and told them the Temple was ready for them to come and pray to God. All the people came. They thanked God for giving them strength to conquer their enemies; they thanked Him for giving them the Temple, where they could worship the One true God; and they sang songs of praise to the Father in Heaven who is so good to all His children, large and small.

Then Judas said:

"Year after year, let us remember this day. It shall be called Chanukkah, the Feast of Lights. Each year, the grown-up people must tell the children this story of how God helped us gain a victory, and of how brave the Jews are. In order that the children may remember better, it will be a good idea if you light little candles in your homes every night for eight nights."

Then the people all went to their homes, and for eight nights they lit the little candles, and told the children the story of Chanukkah.

It is more than two thousand years since all these things took place, but year after year, in December, when Chanukkah comes round, the lights are burning in many Jewish homes. I wish they could be lit in every home and for every child. Then you would remember the heroes who fought the wicked king's soldiers. Then you would love them all, Mattathias and his four brave sons, and the great hero, Judas Maccabee, bravest of all.

XVIII

THE STORY OF PURIM

QUEEN ESTHER

Once upon a time, in the city of Shushan, in Persia, there was a young Jewish girl named Esther. She had no dear parents, for both had died when Esther was very small. She lived with her cousin, Mordecai, who was poor and could not give her any nice dresses to wear. Esther was a very pretty girl. She had two long, thick braids of hair, which hung far down below her waist; she had big black eyes, and the whitest teeth you ever saw.

Mordecai was very kind to the little girl and she was happy. She never thought whether her dresses were fine or plain, and she did not care. She knew her clothes were always clean, and she was careful to keep them so. She loved Mordecai, although she knew he was poor. He had only a very small house, but the room was clean, and they had enough to eat, and had plenty of fresh air.

Their small cottage was on a side street in the city, and not very far away on a fine, wide street, was the palace where the king of Persia lived. The king's name was Ahasuerus. That is a long, hard name, but I think you can read it: A-has-u-e-rus. The king's palace was very large and elegant, and was built out of blocks of pure white marble. The palace stood in the middle of a garden, and all kinds of trees and flowers grew in it. There were some fountains from which the water spouted up into the air, and then fell back into a large basin. If you could have looked into the basin, you would have seen many little fish swimming around all the time.

There was a high wall all around the garden, and there was a heavy gate on the front side, near which was a large tree. No matter how hot the sun shone, it was cool and shady under this tree. Mordecai often took a little stool, set it down near the gate, and sat there in the shade, when he had nothing else to do. The king sometimes saw him seated there, but he was a kind king, and he did not send the old man away.

King Ahasuerus had many soldiers in his palace; many officers were in the rooms to be companions for

THE STORY OF PURIM

the king; he had many men and women to do everything for him, but he was not happy. He had one friend, Prince Haman, who was always with him, but the king was lonesome. He wanted to get married, and he did not know any girl he wished to marry. That made him sad. One day, the king and one of his princes were talking together about it, and the prince said:

"If you do not know any nice young girls, I will tell you how to find some. There are many pretty girls in this big country that belongs to you. All you will have to do, is to send some officers to every town to find the girls, and bring them to Shushan, to the palace."

The king liked this plan and he sent officers to pick out the pretty girls. The officers told the girls the king wanted a wife. The girls were glad to go to Shushan, because every one of them wished she could be the wife of King Ahasuerus.

As one of the officers was going out through the gate, he saw Mordecai and stopped to speak to him. Mordecai asked the officer where he was going, and he answered:

"The king sent me to bring some pretty girls to the

palace. He wants to get married and he does not know any girls. Do you know any who are pretty and sweet and good and kind?"

Mordecai said: "I do not know many girls, but I know one who is kind and good to everybody."

"Who is that girl? Does she live near or far away?" asked the officer.

"Her name is Esther," said Mordecai. "She lives near, and if you would like to see her, I will take you to her home."

The officer said he would go, and Mordecai took him to his own house. Esther had on a very simple cotton dress, but it was neat and clean. When she saw the officer come into the room with Mordecai, she said, with a very pleasant smile:

"Good morning! Won't you please take a seat?"

The officer smiled back at her and said he had no time, but he promised to come again. As he went out of the room, he said to Mordecai:

"I like Esther, because she is sweet and polite. Esther must go to the palace on the day when all the other girls will be there. I will come and get her."

The officer left, and Mordecai said to himself:

THE STORY OF PURIM

"I hope the king will like my Esther, and I hope he will marry her. When she is a queen she can do many things to help the Jews."

Every girl in Persia hoped the king would like her, just her alone, and make her his queen. I mean all the girls except Esther, because she did not know anything at all about it. At last it became known, that on a certain day, all the girls would be in the palace. Then Mordecai told Esther she was to go, too. Esther was bashful, and said to Mordecai:

"Why should I go? I don't think the king will like me. A king wants a tall, splendid girl for his wife, a girl who has fine clothes and a girl who is pretty."

"Do you think so?" said Mordecai.

"Yes I do. I am small, and I am not pretty, and I have no fine clothes."

"Esther, my child, all that does not count. If you are small, you will grow; never mind about being pretty, because maybe the king will think you are pretty; and the king will not care anything about your clothes, if you look neat and clean."

"But I am afraid to go to the palace alone," said Esther.

"Do not be afraid, Esther, for no one will harm you."

At last, when the great day came, Esther was taken into the grand ballroom in the palace. There were, oh! so many girls there, and Esther was told to stand near a window, where the king could see her as soon as he entered the room. Esther had on a cheap little white dress. It was the best she had, but there was no trimming on it. Her long braids were tied with a small blue ribbon. Her cheeks were rosy red, her eyes shone brightly, and when she smiled at the other girls they saw her pretty white teeth.

Esther saw the lovely dresses the other girls wore, but do you think she wished she was dressed like they were? Indeed not. Esther did not worry about what kind of clothes she had. But she liked to see pretty clothes, just as every one else does, and she was happy to look at the handsome silk dresses and the fine lace dresses, and the chains and bracelets and earrings the other girls had. Maybe those girls wondered how it happened that a girl who wore such cheap clothes could have been invited to the palace, and they thought:

"The king will not look at such a poor girl." But they were mistaken.

ESTHER, BEFORE THE KING

THE STORY OF PURIM

The wide doors were thrown open by two soldiers. Several officers, dressed in their gay uniforms, marched in, two by two, and then came the king. He was followed by Haman and many more officers. The king was tall and fine looking. He wore an elegant cloak, embroidered with gold and jewels, over his uniform. His golden crown was on his head and he carried a golden scepter in his hand.

Everybody in the room bowed low, when the king walked to his golden throne and sat down on one of the velvet throne chairs. The other chair remained empty. The king glanced around the room and looked at every girl carefully, but he did not see any one he liked. Then he looked at Esther, standing so bashfully by the window, and said to Haman, who stood beside him:

"Who is that lovely girl with the long braids of hair? I mean the one in that plain white dress."

"Her name is Esther," said Haman. That is all I know about her. But does your majesty really wish to marry her?"

"I certainly do," said the king. "She is the only girl in the room that I like, and I want her for my wife and my queen."

Think of that, children! The great and powerful king did not care for any one of the rich and beautiful girls he saw, and the only girl he liked was Esther. Then the king married her and he gave her handsome clothes to wear, and put a golden crown on her head. He said she was his queen and placed her next to him in the other chair on the throne. Then he gave a feast and invited nearly all the people in Shushan; and there was joy in the land.

One day, Haman asked the king to give an order telling every one to bow down to Haman, whenever they saw him. Mordecai said he would not bow to any one but God. When Haman heard what Mordecai said, he was very angry and said he would punish Mordecai. Haman hated the Jews and he made up his mind to kill all those in Persia. He went to the king and told him Mordecai was a Jew and said:

"The Jews are not good people. They do not pray to our gods and their laws are not like our laws. It is not good for you to have such people in your land."

The king said: "If you tell me the Jews are not good people, of course I believe you; and I will allow you to do anything you like to them."

THE STORY OF PURIM

Then that wicked Haman sent officers to every governor, in every state, with the order from the king that on the thirteenth day of Adar (Adar is a month in the early spring) every Jew was to be killed. Wasn't that terrible?

When Mordecai heard this, he sat by the gate of the palace and cried out loud, and Esther heard him. She sent one of the soldiers to ask what was the matter. Mordecai told the soldier what Haman had done and said:

"Go back and tell Esther all about it. Tell her she must go to the king, and beg him to save her people from being killed."

When the soldier told Esther she said she could only go to the king when the king sent for her. When the soldier told Mordecai that, the old man said:

"Go again to Esther, and tell her she must go to the king. If she does not go, she will be killed the same day as the other Jews."

When Esther heard this, she dressed herself in her best dress and put the golden crown on her head. She looked very beautiful, but she was afraid to go to the king, because he had not sent for her. She stood outside the door of the king's room and she began to tremble and cry. Then she said to herself:

It will not do any good to cry. That will not help any one. I will not cry and I will try to be brave. I will pray to God, and ask Him to make the king kind to me, and let me help my people." So Esther said a little prayer and begged God to help her, and when she had finished her prayers she was not afraid any more, and she went to the king. When he saw her, he smiled at her and held out his golden scepter. She smiled then, because she knew that was a sign that the king was glad to see her. The king asked her what she wanted of him, and Esther said:

"I have been told that on a certain day, the king's soldiers are going to kill all the Jews in Persia."

"That is true," said the king. I gave the order to Haman. Tell me, Esther, why do you ask?"

"Because the Jews are my people and Mordecai is my cousin," said Esther. "I am a Jewish girl, and if all the Jews are to be killed, I will be killed."

Then the king was sorry he had given such an order. He loved Esther and he did not want her to be killed. He asked her what he could do and she said:

THE STORY OF PURIM

"Please give another order to your soldiers. Tell them they must not kill or hurt any Jews."

The king said: "A king in Persia, cannot change any order he has given. I cannot change it, but I will do something else. Go to your cousin Mordecai. Tell him on the day when my soldiers will try to kill the Jews, they should fight the soldiers. I will order the soldiers to let the Jews fight them, and your people will be saved."

Esther thanked the king, and said:

"Prince Haman says he will hang my cousin on a gallows he has just had made."

The king looked at Haman who was in the room, and said angrily:

"I, the king, have been very kind to you, because I thought you were good, but now, I think you are a very wicked man. First you tell me to give an order to kill all the Jews, and then you build a gallows on which to hang Mordecai. The Jews never did you any harm, yet you want to kill them all. You shall be punished."

Haman was frightened when he heard the king call for two officers. They came into the room at once, and the king said: "I have found out that Haman is a very wicked man. Take him away and put him in prison. Tomorrow morning let the soldiers hang him on the same gallows he had built for Mordecai."

Haman fell on his knees before the king. He cried and begged the king to let him live.

"No," said the king. "You would not have saved the life of even one Jew, and I will not let you live. Soldiers, take him away."

Thus was Haman punished. When the day came when the Jews thought Haman was going to have them killed, the soldiers only "made believe" they were fighting, and not one Jew was killed.

The Jews were so happy, they arranged a big feast and they called it Purim. They were so thankful, that they gave presents of food, and clothing, and money, to all the poor men and women and children in the land. All this happened long ago, but each year the Jews remember Purim, and give presents of all kinds to any poor persons they know.